Bash Cookbook

Leverage Bash scripting to automate daily tasks and improve productivity

Ron Brash
Ganesh Naik

BIRMINGHAM - MUMBAI

Bash Cookbook

Commissioning Editor: Vijin Boricha
Acquisition Editor: Rahul Nair
Content Development Editor: Sharon Raj
Technical Editor: Mohit Hassija
Copy Editor: Safis Editing
Project Coordinator: Drashti Panchal
Proofreader: Safis Editing
Indexer: Tejal Daruwale Soni
Graphics: Tom Scaria
Production Coordinator: Shantanu Zagade

First published: July 2018

Production reference: 1300718

Published by Packt Publishing Ltd.
Livery Place
35 Livery Street
Birmingham
B3 2PB, UK.

ISBN 978-1-78862-936-2

www.packtpub.com

mapt.io

Mapt is an online digital library that gives you full access to over 5,000 books and videos, as well as industry leading tools to help you plan your personal development and advance your career. For more information, please visit our website.

Why subscribe?

- Spend less time learning and more time coding with practical eBooks and Videos from over 4,000 industry professionals

- Improve your learning with Skill Plans built especially for you

- Get a free eBook or video every month

- Mapt is fully searchable

- Copy and paste, print, and bookmark content

PacktPub.com

Did you know that Packt offers eBook versions of every book published, with PDF and ePub files available? You can upgrade to the eBook version at www.PacktPub.com and as a print book customer, you are entitled to a discount on the eBook copy. Get in touch with us at service@packtpub.com for more details.

At www.PacktPub.com, you can also read a collection of free technical articles, sign up for a range of free newsletters, and receive exclusive discounts and offers on Packt books and eBooks.

Contributors

About the authors

Ron Brash was the CTO and co-founder of a successful technology consultancy company that provides services in a multitude of domains, but primarily in FOSS and Linux. For over 7 years, he has worked on embedded systems, which provide security and network connectivity in industrial control systems and SCADA networks, all running an optimized embedded Linux. He participates regularly at FOSS and community events, providing feedback and mini-seminars where appropriate. He loves to share knowledge.

Ganesh Naik is an author, consultant, and corporate trainer for embedded Android, embedded Linux, IoT, and ML-related product development. He has over 20 years of experience and project accomplishment in IT. He has been a corporate trainer for Indian Space Research Organization, Intel, GE, Samsung, Motorola, Penang Skills Development Center, and various firms in Singapore and India. He has started a company called Levana Technologies, which works with organizations for consulting and training activities.

About the reviewer

Fabio Alessandro Locati – commonly known as Fale – is a director at Otelia, public speaker, author, and open source contributor. His main areas of expertise are Linux, automation, security, and cloud technologies. Fale has more than 12 years of working experience in IT, with many of them spent consulting for many companies including dozens of Fortune 500 companies. This has allowed him to consider technologies from different points of view, and to develop critical thinking about them.

Packt is searching for authors like you

If you're interested in becoming an author for Packt, please visit `authors.packtpub.com` and apply today. We have worked with thousands of developers and tech professionals, just like you, to help them share their insight with the global tech community. You can make a general application, apply for a specific hot topic that we are recruiting an author for, or submit your own idea.

Table of Contents

Preface   1

Chapter 1: Crash Course in Bash   7
  Getting started with Bash and CLI fundamentals   8
    Your first Bash script with Vim   11
  Creating and using basic variables   13
    Hands-on variable assignment   15
  Hidden Bash variables and reserved words   17
  Conditional logic using if, else, and elseif   19
    Evaluating binary numbers   20
    Evaluating strings   21
    Nested if statements   22
  Case/switch statements and loop constructs   23
    Basic case statement   23
    Basic loops   24
      For loop   24
      Do while loop   25
      Until loop   25
  Using functions and parameters   25
    Using a function with parameters within a for loop   27
  Including source files   27
    Including/importing a library script and using external functions   28
  Retrieving return codes and output   29
    Return code 101   30
  Linking commands, pipes, and input/output   32
    Redirection and pipe bonzanza   34
  Getting program input parameters   35
    Passing your program flags   36
  Getting additional information about commands   38
  Summary   39

Chapter 2: Acting Like a Typewriter and File Explorer   41
  Introduction   41
  Basic searching for strings and files   43
    Getting ready   43
    How to do it...   44
    How it works...   45
  Using wildcards and regexes   47
    Getting ready   49
    How to do it...   49

How it works...   51
Math and calculations in script   55
    Getting ready   56
    How to do it...   57
    How it works...   59
Striping/altering/sorting/deleting/searching strings with Bash only   61
    Getting ready   62
    How to do it...   63
    How it works...   67
Using SED and AWK to remove/replace substrings   70
    Getting ready   71
    How to do it...   71
    How it works...   73
Formatting your data/output using echo and printf   76
    Getting ready   77
    How to do it...   77
    How it works...   79
Readying your script for different languages with internationalization   80
    Getting ready   81
    How to do it...   82
    How it works...   84
Calculating statistics and reducing duplicates based on file contents   87
    Getting ready   88
    How to do it...   88
    How it works...   89
Using file attributes with conditional logic   90
    Getting ready   91
    How to do it...   92
    How it works...   93
Reading delimited data and altered output format   96
    Getting ready   97
    How to do it...   98
    How it works...   99
Chapter 3: Understanding and Gaining File System Mastery   101
  Introduction   101
  Viewing files from various angles – head, tail, less, and more   102
    Getting ready   102
    How to do it...   103
    How it works...   104
  Searching for files by name and/or extension   106
    Getting ready   108
    How to do it...   108
    How it works...   109

Creating a diff of two files and patching   111
Getting ready   112
How to do it...   113
How it works...   114
Creating symbolic links and using them effectively   116
How to do it...   117
How it works...   118
Crawling filesystem directories and printing a tree   119
Getting ready   119
How to do it...   120
How it works...   121
Finding and deleting duplicate files or directories   122
Getting ready   122
How to do it...   123
How it works...   124
Joining and splitting files at arbitrary positions   126
Getting ready   127
How to do it...   127
How it works...   129
Generating datasets and random files of various size   131
Getting ready   132
How to do it...   132
How it works...   134

Chapter 4: Making a Script Behave Like a Daemon   135
Introduction   135
Running a program continuously (forever) using looping constructs or recursion   136
Getting ready   136
How to do it...   137
How it works...   138
Keeping programs/scripts running after logoff   139
Getting ready   140
How to do it...   140
How it works...   141
Invoking commands when they require permissions   142
Getting ready   144
How to do it...   145
How it works...   146
Sanitizing user input and for repeatable results   147
Getting ready   147
How to do it...   148
How it works...   150
Making a simple multi-level user menu using select   151
Getting ready   152

How to do it... 152
How it works... 154
Generating and trapping signals for cleanup 154
Getting ready 155
How to do it... 155
How it works... 156
Using temporary files and lock files in your program 156
Getting ready 157
How to do it... 157
How it works... 158
Leveraging timeout when waiting for command completion 158
Getting ready 159
How to do it... 160
How it works... 161
Creating a file-in-file-out program and running processes in parallel 162
Getting ready 163
How to do it... 163
How it works... 164
Executing your script on startup 165
Getting ready 166
How to do it... 168
How it works... 169

Chapter 5: Scripts for System Administration Tasks 171
Introduction 171
Gathering and aggregating system information 172
Getting ready 172
How to do it... 172
How it works... 174
Gathering network information and connectivity diagnostics 176
Getting ready 176
How to do it... 176
How it works... 177
Configuring basic network connectivity 177
Getting ready 178
How to do it... 178
How it works... 178
Monitoring directories and files 179
Getting ready 179
How to do it... 179
How it works... 179
Compressing and archiving files 179
Getting ready 180
How to do it... 180
How it works... 182

Rotating files from RAM to storage for log rotation — 182
Getting ready — 183
How to do it... — 183
    Adding configuration to /etc/logrotate.d/ — 183
How it works... — 184
Using Linux iptables for a firewall — 184
Getting ready — 185
How to do it... — 185
How it works... — 186
Accessing SQL databases remotely or locally — 186
Getting ready — 186
How to do it... — 186
How it works... — 188
Creating SSH keys for password less remote access — 189
Getting ready — 189
How to do it... — 189
Creating and configuring cron Jobs for task scheduling — 190
How to do it... — 190
How it works... — 191
Creating users and groups systematically — 191
How to do it... — 192
How it works... — 192

Chapter 6: Scripts for Power Users — 193
Introduction — 193
Creating Syslog entries and generating an alarm — 194
Getting ready — 194
How to do it... — 194
How it works... — 195
Backing up and erasing media, disks, and partitions with DD — 196
Getting ready — 196
How to do it... — 196
How it works... — 197
Creating graphics and presentations on the CLI — 197
Getting ready — 197
How to do it... — 197
How it works... — 198
Checking for file integrity and tampering — 199
Getting ready — 199
How to do it... — 199
How it works... — 201
Mounting network file systems and retrieving files — 201
Getting ready — 201
How to do it... — 201
How it works... — 202

Browsing the web from the CLI 202
Getting ready 202
How to do it... 203
How it works... 203
Capturing network traffic headlessly 203
Getting ready 204
How to do it... 204
How it works... 205
Finding binary dependencies 205
Getting ready 205
How to do it... 205
How it works... 206
Fetching time from different locations 206
Getting ready 206
How to do it... 206
How it works... 207
Encrypting/decrypting files from a script 207
Getting ready 207
How to do it... 207
How it works... 208

Chapter 7: Writing Bash to Win and Profit 209
Introduction 209
Creating a lame utility HTTP server 210
Getting ready 210
How to do it... 210
How it works... 211
Parsing RSS feeds and output HTML 211
Getting ready 211
How to do it... 211
How it works... 211
Scraping the web and collecting files 212
Getting ready 212
How to do it... 212
How it works... 212
Making a simple IRC chat bot logger 213
Getting ready 213
How to do it... 213
How it works... 214
Blocking IP addresses from failed SSH attempts 214
Getting ready 214
How to do it... 214
How it works... 215
Playing and managing audio from Bash 215
Getting ready 215

How to do it...   215
How it works...   216
Creating a simple NAT and DMZ firewall   216
Getting ready   216
How to do it...   216
How it works...   217
Parsing a GitHub project and generate a report   217
Getting ready   217
How to do it...   217
How it works...   218
Creating a poor man's incremental remote backup   218
Getting ready   218
How to do it...   218
How it works...   219
Using Bash scripts to monitor udev input   219
Getting ready   219
How to do it...   219
How it works...   220
Using Bash to monitor battery life and optimize it   220
Getting ready   220
How to do it...   220
How it works...   221
Using chroot and restricted Bash shells to secure scripts   222
Getting ready   222
How to do it...   222
How it works...   222

Chapter 8: Advanced Scripting Techniques   223
Introduction   223
Calculating and reducing the runtime of a script   224
Getting ready   224
How to do it...   224
How it works...   224
Writing one-line conditional statements and loops   224
Getting ready   225
How to do it...   225
How it works...   225
**Avoiding command not found warnings/errors and improving
portability**   226
Getting ready   226
How to do it...   226
How it works...   227
Creating a config file and using it in tandem with your scripts   227
Getting ready   227
How to do it...   227

How it works...   228
Improving your shell – GCC and command line colors   228
Getting ready   228
How to do it...   229
How it works...   230
Adding aliases, and altering user paths/variables   230
Getting ready   231
How to do it...   231
How it works...   231
Echoing output to raw terminal devices   231
Getting ready   231
How to do it...   232
How it works...   232
Creating simple frontend GUIs for Bash scripts   232
Getting ready   233
How to do it...   233
How it works...   235
Compiling and installing your own Bash shell   235
Getting ready   236
How to do it...   236
How it works...   236
Recording terminal sessions for automation   237
Getting ready   237
How to do it...   237
How it works...   237
Writing high-quality scripts by example   237
Getting ready   238
How to do it...   238
How it works...   238

Other Books You May Enjoy   239

Index   243

Preface

In this book, we are writing a variety of scripts using **Bash**, or the **Bourne Again Shell**. They range from simple to more complex and handy utilities or programs. Currently, Bash is the default shell used by most GNU/Linux distributions and is used ubiquitously within the Linux Terminal. It can be used for any number of tasks and is flexible across the Linux/Unix ecosystem. In other words, a user familiar with Bash and the Linux CLI can install it themselves on almost any other Linux system and perform similar tasks with a negligible amount of alterations (if any are required at all). Bash scripts can also still work with few dependencies on other software installed, and on a very lean system (minimal installation), a user can still write a powerful script to automate tasks or assist with repeated task execution.

This cookbook focuses entirely on Bash usage in an Ubuntu environment, a very common Linux distribution, but it should be portable to other distributions with relative ease. This book is not written for direct usage on Apple or Windows OSes even though it is possible to port elements over to them.

Who this book is for

Bash Cookbook is for power users or system administrators who are involved in writing Bash scripts in order to automate tasks or are aiming to enhance their productivity on the command line. For example, instead of remembering a series of commands to perform a specific operation, all of those commands can be put into a single script dedicated to that task, and they can perform input validation and format output. Why not save time and reduce errors through a powerful tool?

This book is also ideal if you are interested in learning how to automate complex daily system tasks that can be executed by various system infrastructure such as starting a script on system boot, or through scheduled cron jobs.

What this book covers

Chapter 1, *Crash Course in Bash*, covers the Linux shell/Bash to get you up and running, and the remainder of the book will just fall into place.

Chapter 2, *Acting Like a Typewriter and File Explorer*, introduces several bolt-on technologies to make Bash even more extensive when searching for items and text, or automating file explorer/filesystem operations.

Chapter 3, *Understanding and Gaining File System Mastery*, will help you view files from various angles: head, tail, less, searching for files by name and/or extension, creating a diff of two files, patching, creating symbolic links and using them effectively, crawling filesystem directories, printing a tree, and more.

Chapter 4, *Making a Script Behave Like a Daemon*, is about creating components that mimic application functionality, such as menus or a daemon.

Chapter 5, *Scripts for System Administration Tasks*, introduces logs, archiving them, job/task management, network connectivity, securing systems using a firewall (iptables), monitoring directories for changes, and creating users.

Chapter 6, *Scripts for Power Users*, is about creating syslog entries using the logger command, taking backups, creating graphics and presentations on the CLI, checking file integrity and tampering, mounting network filesystems, retrieving files, browsing the Web, capturing network traffic, finding binary dependencies, and encrypting and decrypting a file.

Chapter 7, *Writing Bash to Win and Profit*, will help you learn how to use commands and scripts for many tasks. You will get an idea about writing bash scripts for monitoring certain tasks.

Chapter 8, *Advanced Scripting Techniques*, will help you learn about advanced scripting techniques as well as how to customize their shell.

To get the most out of this book

As the authors, we wrote this book to be accessible and teach you, the reader many different approaches to programming with Bash through several recipes. However, to get the most out of them, we encourage you to:

- Have a Linux system setup and configured (ideally Ubuntu) to complete the recipes
- Work through the recipes
- Keep in mind what the components of each recipe and even the recipes themselves to see how they could be reused or combined in new ways

However, this book assumes a certain level of knowledge to begin your journey and these skills will not be covered in this book. These skills include the following:

- How to setup and configure a Linux system
- How to install, access, and configure a specific text editor (although several are already included in most Linux distributions)
- Some basics about computing and programming (although we will do our best to provide a crash course)

To gain proficiency in those areas, we recommend that you either give it your best shot if you are an adept problem solver and quick learner, or checkout the following resources first:

- Linux or distribution communities
- Open source forums or groups
- YouTube or similar media

Download the example code files

You can download the example code files for this book from your account at www.packtpub.com. If you purchased this book elsewhere, you can visit www.packtpub.com/support and register to have the files emailed directly to you.

You can download the code files by following these steps:

1. Log in or register at `www.packtpub.com`.
2. Select the **SUPPORT** tab.
3. Click on **Code Downloads & Errata**.
4. Enter the name of the book in the **Search** box and follow the onscreen instructions.

Once the file is downloaded, please make sure that you unzip or extract the folder using the latest version of:

- WinRAR/7-Zip for Windows
- Zipeg/iZip/UnRarX for Mac
- 7-Zip/PeaZip for Linux

The code bundle for the book is also hosted on GitHub at `https://github.com/PacktPublishing/Bash-Cookbook`. In case, there's an update to the code, it will be updated on the existing GitHub repository.

We also have other code bundles from our rich catalog of books and videos available at `https://github.com/PacktPublishing/`. Check them out!

Conventions used

There are a number of text conventions used throughout this book.

`CodeInText`: Indicates code words in text, database table names, folder names, filenames, file extensions, pathnames, dummy URLs, user input, and Twitter handles. Here is an example: "The full path is more concrete and hardcoded; the interpreter will try to use the complete path. For example, `/bin/ls or /usr/local/bin/myBinary`.."

A block of code is set as follows:

```
#!/bin/bash
AGE=17
if [ ${AGE} -lt 18 ]; then
    echo "You must be 18 or older to see this movie"
fi
```

Any command-line input or output is written as follows:

```
rbrash@moon:~$ history
1002 ls
1003 cd ../
1004 pwd
1005 whoami
1006 history
```

Bold: Indicates a new term, an important word, or words that you see onscreen. For example, words in menus or dialog boxes appear in the text like this.

Warnings or important notes appear like this.

Tips and tricks appear like this.

Sections

In this book, you will find several headings that appear frequently (*Getting ready, How to do it..., How it works..., There's more...*, and *See also*).

To give clear instructions on how to complete a recipe, use these sections as follows:

Getting ready

This section tells you what to expect in the recipe and describes how to set up any software or any preliminary settings required for the recipe.

How to do it...

This section contains the steps required to follow the recipe.

How it works...

This section usually consists of a detailed explanation of what happened in the previous section.

There's more...

This section consists of additional information about the recipe in order to make you more knowledgeable about the recipe.

See also

This section provides helpful links to other useful information for the recipe.

Get in touch

Feedback from our readers is always welcome.

General feedback: Email `feedback@packtpub.com` and mention the book title in the subject of your message. If you have questions about any aspect of this book, please email us at `questions@packtpub.com`.

Errata: Although we have taken every care to ensure the accuracy of our content, mistakes do happen. If you have found a mistake in this book, we would be grateful if you would report this to us. Please visit `www.packtpub.com/submit-errata`, selecting your book, clicking on the Errata Submission Form link, and entering the details.

Piracy: If you come across any illegal copies of our works in any form on the internet, we would be grateful if you would provide us with the location address or website name. Please contact us at `copyright@packtpub.com` with a link to the material.

If you are interested in becoming an author: If there is a topic that you have expertise in and you are interested in either writing or contributing to a book, please visit `authors.packtpub.com`.

Reviews

Please leave a review. Once you have read and used this book, why not leave a review on the site that you purchased it from? Potential readers can then see and use your unbiased opinion to make purchase decisions, we at Packt can understand what you think about our products, and our authors can see your feedback on their book. Thank you!

For more information about Packt, please visit `packtpub.com`.

Crash Course in Bash 1

The primary purpose of this chapter is to give you enough knowledge about the Linux shell/Bash to get you up and running, as that the remainder of the book will just fall into place.

In this chapter, we will cover the following topics:

- Getting started with Bash and CLI fundamentals
- Creating and using basic variables
- Hidden Bash variables and reserved words
- Conditional logic using if, else, and elseif
- Case/switch statements and loop constructs
- Using functions and parameters
- Including source files
- Parsing program input parameters
- Standard in, standard out, and standard error
- Linking commands using pipes
- Finding more information about the commands used within Bash

 This chapter will set you up with the basic knowledge needed to complete the recipes in the remaining chapters of the book.

Getting started with Bash and CLI fundamentals

First, we need to open a Linux terminal or shell. Depending on your flavor (distribution) of Linux, this will be done in one of several ways, but in Ubuntu, the easiest way is to navigate to the **Applications** menu and find one labeled terminal. The terminal or shell is the place where commands are entered by a user and executed in the same shell. Simply put, results (if any) are displayed, and the terminal will remain open, waiting for new commands to be entered. Once a shell has been opened, a *prompt* will appear, looking similar to the following:

```
rbrash@moon:~$
```

The prompt will be in the format of your `username@YourComputersHostName` followed by a delimiter. Throughout this cookbook, you will see commands with the user `rbrash`; this is short for the author's name (Ron Brash) and in you case, it will match your username.

It may also look similar to:

```
root@hostname #
```

The `$` refers to a regular user and the `#` refers to root. In the Linux and Unix worlds, root refers to the *root user*, which is similar to the Windows Administrator user. It can be used to perform any manner of tasks, so caution should be used when using a user with root privileges. For example, the root user can access all files on the OS, and can also be used to delete any or all critical files used by the OS, which could render the system unusable or broken.

When a terminal or shell is run, the Bash shell is executed with a set of parameters and commands specific to the user's bash profile. This profile is often called the `.bashrc` and can be used to contain command aliases, shortcuts, environment variables, and other user enhancements, such as prompt colors. It is located at `~/.bashrc` or `~/.bash_profile`.

 `~ or ~/` is a shortcut for your user's home directory. It is synonymous with `/home/yourUserName/`, and for root, it is `/root`.

Your user's Bash shell also contains a history of all of the commands run by the user (located in `~/.bash_history`), which can be accessed using the `history` command, shown as follows:

```
rbrash@moon:~$ history
1002 ls
1003 cd ../
1004 pwd
1005 whoami
1006 history
```

For example, your first command might be to use `ls` to determine the contents of the directory. The command `cd` is used to change the directory, to one directory in above the parent directory. The `pwd` command is used to return the complete path to the working directory (for example, where the terminal is currently navigated to).

Another command you may execute on the shell might be the `whoami` command, which will return the user currently logged in to the shell:

```
rbrash@moon:/$ whoami
rbrash
rbrash@moon:/$
```

Using the concept of entering commands, we can put those (or any) commands into a *shell script*. In its most simplistic representation, a shell script looks like the following:

```
#!/bin/bash
# Pound or hash sign signifies a comment (a line that is not executed)
whoami       #Command returning the current username
pwd          #Command returning the current working directory on the
filesystem
ls           # Command returning the results (file listing) of the current
working directory
echo "Echo one 1"; echo "Echo two 2" # Notice the semicolon used to delimit
multiple commands in the same execution.
```

The first line contains the path to the interpreter and tells the shell which interpreter to use when interpreting this script. The first line will *always* contain the shebang (`#!`) and the prefix to the path appended without a space:

```
#!/bin/bash
```

A script cannot execute by itself; it needs to be executed by a user or to be *called* by another program, the system, or another script. The execution of a script also requires it to have *executable* permissions, which can be granted by a user so that it can become executable; this can be done with the `chmod` command.

To add or *grant* basic executable permissions, use the following command:

```
$ chmod a+x script.sh
```

To execute the script, one of the following methods can be used:

```
$ bash script.sh        # if the user is currently in the same directory
as the script
$ bash /path/to/script.sh # Full path
```

If the correct permissions are applied, and the shebang and Bash interpreter path is correct, you may alternatively use the following two commands to execute `script.sh`:

```
$ ./script.sh # if the user is currently in the same directory as the
script
$ /path/to/script.sh # Full path
```

From the preceding command snippets, you might notice a few things regarding paths. The path to a script, file, or executable can be referred to using a *relative* address and a `full path`. Relative addressing effectively tells the interpreter to execute whatever may exist in the current directory or using the user's global shell `$PATH` variables. For example, the system knows that binaries or executable binaries are stored in `/usr/bin`, `/bin/` and `/sbin` and will look there first. The full path is more concrete and *hardcoded*; the interpreter will try to use the complete path. For example, `/bin/ls` or `/usr/local/bin/myBinary`.

When you are looking to run a binary in the directory you are currently working in, you can use either `./script.sh`, bash `script.sh`, or even the full path. Obviously, there are advantages and disadvantages to each approach.

Hardcoded or full paths can be useful when you know exactly where a binary may reside on a specific system and you cannot rely on `$PATH` variables for potential security or system configuration reasons. Relative paths are useful when flexibility is required. For example, program `ABC` could be in location `/usr/bin` or in `/bin`, but it could be called simply with `ABC` instead of `/pathTo/ABC`.

So far, we have covered what a basic Bash script looks like, and briefly introduced a few very basic, but essential commands and paths. However, to create a script—you need an editor! In Ubuntu, usually by default, you have a few editors available to you for the creation of a Bash script: vi/vim, nano, and gedit. There are a number of other text editors or **integrated development editors (IDEs)** available, but this is a personal choice and up to the reader to find one they like. All of the examples and recipes in this book can be followed regardless of the text editor chosen.

Without using a full-blown editor such as the popular Eclipse, Emacs or Geany may also be useful as flexible IDEs within resource-constrained environments, for example, a Raspberry Pi.

Knowledge of vi/vim and nano is very handy when you want to create or modify a script remotely over SSH and on the console. Vi/vim may seem a bit archaic, but it saves the day when your favorite editor is not installed or cannot be accessed.

Your first Bash script with Vim

Let's start by creating a script using improved version of vi (called vim). If Vim (VI-enhanced) is not installed, it can be installed with sudo or root using the following command (-y is short for yes):

```
For Ubuntu or Debian based distributions
$ sudo apt-get -y install vim
For CentOS or RHEL
$ sudo yum install -y vim
For Fedora
$ sudo dnf install -y vim
```

Open a terminal and enter the following commands to first see where your terminal is currently navigated to, and to create the script using vim:

```
$ pwd
/home/yourUserName
$ vim my_first_script.sh
```

The terminal window will transform into the Vim application (similar to the following screenshot) and you will be just about ready to program your first script. Simultaneously press the *Esc+ I* keys to enter Insert mode; there will be an indicator in the bottom left and the cursor block will begin to flash:

To navigate Vim, you may use any number of keyboard shortcuts, but the arrow keys are the simplest to move the cursor up, down, left, and right. Move the cursor to the beginning of the first line and type the following:

```
#!/bin/bash
# Echo this is my first comment
echo "Hello world! This is my first Bash script!"
echo -n "I am executing the script with user: "
whoami
echo -n "I am currently running in the directory: "
pwd
exit 0
```

We have already introduced the concept of a comment and a few basic commands, but we have yet to introduce the flexible `echo` command. The `echo` command can be used to print text to the console or into files, and the `-n` flag prints text without the end line character (end line has the same effect as pressing *Enter* on the keyboard)—this allows the output from the `whoami` and `pwd` commands to appear on the same line.

The program also exits with a status of 0, which means that it exited with a normal status. This will be covered later as we move toward searching or checking command exit statuses for errors and other conditions.

When you've finished, press *Esc* to exit insert mode; going back to command mode and typing : will allow you to write the vim command *w + q*. In summary, type the following key sequence: *Esc* and then *:wq*. This will exit Vim by writing to disk (w) and quitting (q), and will return you to the console.

 More information about Vim can be obtained by reviewing its documentation using the Linux manual pages or by referring to a sibling book available from Packt (`https://www.packtpub.com/application-development/hacking-vim-72`).

To execute your first script, enter the `bash my_first_script.sh` command and the console will return a similar output:

```
$ bash my_first_script.sh
Hello world! This is my first Bash script!
I am executing the script with user: rbrash
I am currently running in the directory: /home/rbrash
$
```

Congratulations—you have created and executed your first Bash script. With these skills, you can begin creating more complex scripts to automate and simplify just about any daily CLI routines.

Creating and using basic variables

The best way to think of variables is as placeholders for values. They can be permanent (static) or transient (dynamic), and they will have a concept called **scope** (more on this later). To get ready to use variables, we need to think about the script you just wrote: `my_first_script.sh`. In the script, we could have easily used variables to contain values that are static (there every time) or dynamic ones created by running commands every time the script is run. For example, if we would like to use a value such as the value of `PI` (3.14), then we could use a variable like this short script snippet:

```
PI=3.14
echo "The value of PI is $PI"
```

If included in a full script, the script snippet would output:

```
The value of Pi is 3.14
```

Notice that the idea of setting a value (3.14) to a variable is called assignment. We *assigned* the value of 3.14 to a variable with the name PI. We also referred to the PI variable using $PI. This can be achieved in a number of ways:

```
echo "1. The value of PI is $PI"
echo "2. The value of PI is ${PI}"
echo "3. The value of PI is" $PI
```

This will output the following:

```
1. The value of PI is 3.14
2. The value of PI is 3.14
3. The value of PI is 3.14
```

While the output is identical, the mechanisms are slightly different. In version 1, we refer to the PI variable within double quotes, which indicates a **string (an array of characters)**. We could also use single quotes, but this would make this a **literal string**. In version 2, we refer to the variable inside of { } or *squiggly* brackets; this is useful for protecting the variable in cases where this would break the script. The following is an example:

```
echo "1. The value of PI is $PIabc" # Since PIabc is not declared, it will
be empty string
echo "2. The value of PI is ${PI}"  # Still works because we correctly
referred to PI
```

If any variable is not declared and then we try to use it, that variable will be initialized to an empty string.

The following command will convert a numeric value to a string representation. In our example, $PI is still a variable containing a number, but we could have created the PI variable like this as well:

```
PI="3.14" # Notice the double quotes ""
```

This would contain within the variable a string and not a numeric value such as **an integer or float**.

The concept of data types is not explored to its fullest in this cookbook. It is best left as a topic for the reader to explore, as it is a fundamental concept of programming and computer usage.

Wait! You say there is a difference between a number and a string? Absolutely, because without conversion (or being set correctly in the first place), this may limit the things you can do with it. For example, 3.14 is not the same as 3.14 (the number). 3.14 is made up of four characters: 3 + . + 1 +4. If we wanted to perform multiplication on our PI value in string form, either the calculation/script would break or we would get a nonsensical answer.

 We will talk more about conversion later, in Chapter 2, *Acting like a Typewriter and File Explorer.*

Let's say we want to assign one variable to another. We would do this like so:

```
VAR_A=10
VAR_B=$VAR_A
VAR_C=${VAR_B}
```

If the preceding snippet were within a functioning Bash script, we would get the value 10 for each variable.

Hands-on variable assignment

Open a new blank file and add the following to it:

```
#!/bin/bash

PI=3.14
VAR_A=10
VAR_B=$VAR_A
VAR_C=${VAR_B}

echo "Let's print 3 variables:"
echo $VAR_A
echo $VAR_B
echo $VAR_C

echo "We know this will break:"
echo "0. The value of PI is $PIabc"     # since PIabc is not declared, it
will be empty string

echo "And these will work:"
echo "1. The value of PI is $PI"
echo "2. The value of PI is ${PI}"
echo "3. The value of PI is" $PI
```

```
echo "And we can make a new string"
STR_A="Bob"
STR_B="Jane"
echo "${STR_A} + ${STR_B} equals Bob + Jane"
STR_C=${STR_A}" + "${STR_B}
echo "${STR_C} is the same as Bob + Jane too!"
echo "${STR_C} + ${PI}"

exit 0
```

Notice the nomenclature. It is great to use a standardized mechanism to name variables, but to use STR_A and VAR_B is clearly not descriptive enough if used multiple times. In the future, we will use more descriptive names, such as VAL_PI to mean the value of PI or STR_BOBNAME to mean the string representing Bob's name. In Bash, capitalization is often used to describe variables, as it adds clarity.

Press **Save** and exit to a terminal (open one if one isn't already open). Execute your script after applying the appropriate permissions, and you should see the following output:

```
Lets print 3 variables:
10
10
10
We know this will break:
0. The value of PI is
And these will work:
1. The value of PI is 3.14
2. The value of PI is 3.14
3. The value of PI is 3.14
And we can make a new string
Bob + Jane equals Bob + Jane
Bob + Jane is the same as Bob + Jane too!
Bob + Jane + 3.14
```

First, we saw how we can use three variables, assign values to each of then, and print them. Secondly, we saw through a demonstration that the interpreter can break when concatenating strings (let's keep this in mind). Thirdly, we printed out our PI variable and concatenated it to a string using echo. Finally, we performed a few more types of concatenation, including a final version, which converts a numeric value and appends it to a string.

Hidden Bash variables and reserved words

Wait—there are hidden variables and reserved words? Yes! There are words you can't use in your script unless properly contained in a construct such as a string. Global variables are available in a **global context**, which means that they are visible to all scripts in the current shell or open shell consoles. In a later chapter, we will explore global shell variables more, but just so you're aware, know that there are useful variables available for you to reuse, such as $USER, $PWD, $OLDPWD, and $PATH.

To see a list of all shell environment variables, you can use the env command (the output has been cut short):

```
$ env
XDG_VTNR=7
XDG_SESSION_ID=c2
CLUTTER_IM_MODULE=xim
XDG_GREETER_DATA_DIR=/var/lib/lightdm-data/rbrash
SESSION=ubuntu
SHELL=/bin/bash
TERM=xterm-256color
XDG_MENU_PREFIX=gnome-
VTE_VERSION=4205
QT_LINUX_ACCESSIBILITY_ALWAYS_ON=1
WINDOWID=81788934
UPSTART_SESSION=unix:abstract=/com/ubuntu/upstart-session/1000/1598
GNOME_KEYRING_CONTROL=
GTK_MODULES=gail:atk-bridge:unity-gtk-module
USER=rbrash
....
```

 Modifying the PATH environment variable can be very useful. It can also be frustrating, because it contains the filesystem path to binaries. For example, you have binaries in /bin or /sbin or /usr/bin, but when you run a single command, the command is run without you specifying the path.

Alright, so we have acknowledged the existence of pre-existing variables and that there could be new global variables created by the user or other programs. When using variables that have a high probability of being similarly named, be careful to make them specific to your application.

In addition to hidden variables, there are also words that are reserved for use within a script or shell. For example, if and else are words that are used to provide conditional logic to scripts. Imagine if you created a command, variable, or function (more later on this) with the same name as one that already exists? The script would likely break or run an erroneous operation.

When trying to avoid any naming collisions (or namespace collisions), try to make your variables more likely to be used by your application by appending or prefixing an identifier that is likely to be unique.

The following list contains some of the more common reserved words that you will encounter. Some of which are likely to look very familiar because they tell the Bash interpreter to interpret any text in a specific way, redirect output, run an application in the background, or are even used in other programming/scripting languages.

- `if`, `elif`, `else`, `fi`
- `while`, `do`, `for`, `done`, `continue`, `break`
- `case`, `select`, `time`
- `function`
- `&`, `|`, `>`, `<`, `!`, `=`
- `#`, `$`, `(`, `)`, `;`, `{`, `}`, `[`, `]`, `\`

For the full reference, go to: `https://www.gnu.org/software/bash/manual/html_node/Reserved-Word-Index.html`.

The last element in the list contains an array of specific characters that tell Bash to perform specific functionalities. The pound sign signifies a comment for example. However, the backslash \ is very special because it is an **escape character**. Escape characters are used to *escape* or *stop* the interpreter from executing specific functionality when it sees those particular characters. For example:

```
$ echo # Comment

$ echo \# Comment
# Comment
```

Escaping characters will become very useful in Chapter 2, *Acting like a Typewriter and File Explorer*, when working with strings and single/double quotes.

The escape character prevents the execution of the next character after the forward slash. However, this is not necessarily consistent when working with carriage returns (\n, \r\n) and null bytes (\0).

Conditional logic using if, else, and elseif

The previous section introduced the concept that there are several reserved words and a number of characters that have an effect on the operation of Bash. The most basic, and probably most widely used conditional logic is with `if` and `else` statements. Let's use an example code snippet:

```
#!/bin/bash
AGE=17
if [ ${AGE} -lt 18 ]; then
 echo "You must be 18 or older to see this movie"
fi
```

 Notice the space after or before the square brackets in the `if` statement. Bash is particularly picky about the syntax of bracketing.

If we are evaluating the variable `age` using less than (<) or `-lt` (Bash offers a number of syntactical constructs for evaluating variables), we need to use an `if` statement. In our `if` statement, if `$AGE` is less than 18, we echo the message `You must be 18 or older to see this movie`. Otherwise, the script will not execute the `echo` statement and will continue execution. Notice that the `if` statement ends with the reserved word `fi`. This is not a mistake and is required by Bash syntax.

Let's say we want to add a catchall using `else`. If the `then` command block of the `if` statement is not satisfied, then the `else` will be executed:

```
#!/bin/bash
AGE=40
if [ ${AGE} -lt 18 ]
then
    echo "You must be 18 or older to see this movie"
else
    echo "You may see the movie!"
    exit 1
fi
```

With AGE set to the integer value 40, the then command block inside the if statement will not be satisfied and the else command block will be executed.

Evaluating binary numbers

Let's say we want to introduce another if condition and use elif (short for *else if*):

```
#!/bin/bash
AGE=21
if [ ${AGE} -lt 18 ]; then
  echo "You must be 18 or older to see this movie"
elif [ ${AGE} -eq 21 ]; then
  echo "You may see the movie and get popcorn"
else
  echo "You may see the movie!"
  exit 1
fi

echo "This line might not get executed"
```

If AGE is set and equals 21, then the snippet will echo:

```
You may see the movie and get popcorn
This line might not get executed
```

Using if, elif, and else, combined with other evaluations, we can execute specific branches of logic and functions or even exit our script. To evaluate raw binary variables, use the following **operators**:

- -gt (greater than >)
- -ge (greater or equal to >=)
- -lt (less than <)
- -le (less than or equal to <=)
- -eq (equal to)
- -nq (not equal to)

Evaluating strings

As mentioned in the variables subsection, numeric values are different from strings. Strings are typically evaluated like this:

```bash
#!/bin/bash
MY_NAME="John"
NAME_1="Bob"
NAME_2="Jane"
NAME_3="Sue"
Name_4="Kate"

if [ "${MY_NAME}" == "Ron" ]; then
    echo "Ron is home from vacation"
elif [ "${MY_NAME}" != ${NAME_1}" && "${MY_NAME}" != ${NAME_2}" &&
"${MY_NAME}" == "John" ]; then
    echo "John is home after some unnecessary AND logic"
elif [ "${MY_NAME}" == ${NAME_3}" || "${MY_NAME}" == ${NAME_4}" ]; then
    echo "Looks like one of the ladies are home"
else
    echo "Who is this stranger?"
fi
```

In the preceding snippet, you might notice that the MY_NAME variable will be executed and the string John is home after some unnecessary AND logic will be echoed to the console. In the snippet, the logic flows like this:

1. If MY_NAME is equal to Ron, then echo "Ron is home from vacation"
2. Else if MY_NAME is not equal to NAME_1 **AND** MY_NAME is not equal to NAME_2 **AND** MY_NAME is equal to John, then echo "John is home after some unnecessary AND logic"
3. Else if MY_NAME is equal to NAME_3 **OR** MY_NAME is equal to NAME_4, then echo "Looks like one of the ladies"
4. Else echo "Who is this stranger?"

Notice the operators: &&, ||, ==, and !=

- && (means and)
- || (means or)
- == (is equal to)
- != (not equal to)
- -n (is not null or is not set)
- -z (is null and zero length)

Null means not set or empty in the world of computing. There are many different types of operators or tests that can be used in your scripts. For more information, check out: http://tldp.org/LDP/abs/html/comparison-ops.html and https:/ /www.gnu.org/software/bash/manual/html_node/Shell-Arithmetic. html#Shell-Arithmetic

You can also evaluate numbers as if they are strings using (("$a" > "$b")) or [["$a" > "$b"]]. Notice the usage of double parentheses and square brackets.

Nested if statements

If a single level of if statements is not enough and you would like to have additional logic within an if statement, you can create **nested conditional statements**. This can be done in the following way:

```
#!/bin/bash
USER_AGE=18
AGE_LIMIT=18
NAME="Bob" # Change to your username if you want to execute the nested
logic
HAS_NIGHTMARES="true"

if [ "${USER}" == "${NAME}" ]; then
    if [ ${USER_AGE} -ge ${AGE_LIMIT} ]; then
        if [ "${HAS_NIGHTMARES}" == "true" ]; then
            echo "${USER} gets nightmares, and should not see the movie"
        fi
    fi
else
    echo "Who is this?"
fi
```

Case/switch statements and loop constructs

Besides if and else statements, Bash offers case or switch statements and loop constructs that can be used to simplify logic so that it is more readable and sustainable. Imagine creating an if statement with many elif evaluations. It would become cumbersome!

```
#!/bin/bash
VAR=10

# Multiple IF statements
if [ $VAR -eq 1 ]; then
    echo "$VAR"
elif [ $VAR -eq 2]; then
    echo "$VAR"
elif [ $VAR -eq 3]; then
    echo "$VAR"
# .... to 10
else
    echo "I am not looking to match this value"
fi
```

In a large number of blocks of conditional logic of if and elifs, each if and elif needs to be evaluated before executing a specific branch of code. It can be faster to use a case/switch statement, because the first match will be executed (and it looks prettier).

Basic case statement

Instead of if/else statements, you can use **case statements** to evaluate a variable. Notice that esac is case backwards and is used to exit the case statement similar to fi for if statements.

Case statements follow this flow:

```
case $THING_I_AM_TO_EVALUATE in
  1) # Condition to evaluate is number 1 (could be "a" for a string too!)
    echo "THING_I_AM_TO_EVALUATE equals 1"
    ;; # Notice that this is used to close this evaluation
  *) # * Signified the catchall (when THING_I_AM_TO_EVALUATE does not equal
values in the switch)
    echo "FALLTHOUGH or default condition"
esac # Close case statement
```

The following is a working example:

```
#!/bin/bash
VAR=10 # Edit to 1 or 2 and re-run, after running the script as is.
case $VAR in
  1)
    echo "1"
    ;;
  2)
    echo "2"
    ;;
  *)
    echo "What is this var?"
    exit 1
esac
```

Basic loops

Can you imagine iterating through a list of files or a dynamic array and monotonously evaluating each and every one? Or waiting until a condition was true? For these types of scenarios, you may want to use a **for loop, a do while loop, or an until loop** to improve your script and make things easy. For loops, do while loops, and until loops may seem similar, but there are subtle differences between them.

For loop

The for loop is usually used when you have multiple tasks or commands to execute for each of the entries in an array or *want to execute a given command on a finite number of items*. In this example, we have an array (or list) containing three elements: file1, file2, and file3. The for loop will echo each element within FILES and exit the script:

```
#!/bin/bash

FILES=( "file1" "file2" "file3" )
for ELEMENT in ${FILES[@]}
do
        echo "${ELEMENT}"
done

echo "Echo\'d all the files"
```

Do while loop

As an alternative, we have included the `do while` loop. It is similar to a `for` loop, but better suited to *dynamic conditions*, such as when you do not know when a value will be returned or performing a task until a condition is met. The condition within the square brackets is the same as an *if* statement:

```
#!/bin/bash
CTR=1
while [ ${CTR} -lt 9 ]
do
    echo "CTR var: ${CTR}"
    ((CTR++)) # Increment the CTR variable by 1
done
echo "Finished"
```

Until loop

For completeness, we have included the `until` loop. It is not used very often and is almost the same as a `do while` loop. Notice that its condition and operation is consistent with incrementing a counter `until` a value is reached:

```
#!/bin/bash
CTR=1
until [ ${CTR} -gt 9 ]
do
    echo "CTR var: ${CTR}"
    ((CTR++)) # Increment the CTR variable by 1
done
echo "Finished"
```

Using functions and parameters

So far in the book, we have mentioned that function is a reserved word and only used in Bash scripts that are in a single procedure, but what is a function?

To illustrate what a function is, first we need to define what a function is—a **function** is a self-contained section of code that performs a single task. However, a function performing a task may also execute many subtasks in order to complete its main task.

For example, you could have a function called `file_creator` that performs the following tasks:

1. Check to see whether a file exists.
2. If the file exists, truncate it. Otherwise, create a new one.
3. Apply the correct permissions.

A function can also be passed parameters. **Parameters** are like variables that can be set outside of a function and then used within the function itself. This is really useful because we can create segments of code that perform generic tasks that are reusable by other scripts or even within loops themselves. You may also have **local** variables that are not accessible outside of a function and for usage only within the function itself. So what does a function look like?

```
#!/bin/bash
function my_function() {
    local PARAM_1="$1"
    local PARAM_2="$2"
    local PARAM_3="$3"
    echo "${PARAM_1} ${PARAM_2} ${PARAM_3}"
}
my_function "a" "b" "c"
```

As we can see in the simple script, there is a function declared as `my_function` using the `function` reserved word. The content of the function is contained within the squiggly brackets `{ }` and introduces three new concepts:

- **Parameters** are referred to systematically like this: `$1` for parameter 1, `$2` for parameter 2, `$3` for parameter 3, and so on
- The `local` keyword refers to the fact that variables *declared* with this keyword remain accessible only within this function
- We can call functions merely by name and use parameters simply by adding them, as in the preceding example

In the next section, we'll dive into a more realistic example that should drive the point home a bit more: functions are helpful everyday and make functionality from any section easily reusable where appropriate.

Using a function with parameters within a for loop

In this short example, we have a function called `create_file`, which is called within a loop for each file in the `FILES` array. The function creates a file, modifies its permissions, and then passively checks for its existence using the `ls` command:

```
#!/bin/bash
FILES=( "file1" "file2" "file3" ) # This is a global variable

function create_file() {
    local FNAME="${1}" # First parameter
    local PERMISSIONS="${2}" # Second parameter
    touch "${FNAME}"
    chmod "${PERMISSIONS}" "${FNAME}"
    ls -l "${FNAME}"
}

for ELEMENT in ${FILES[@]}
do
        create_file "${ELEMENT}" "a+x"
done

echo "Created all the files with a function!"
exit 0
```

Including source files

In addition to functions, we can also create multiple scripts and include them such that we can utilize any shared variables of functions.

Let's say we have a library or utility script that contains a number of functions useful for creating files. This script by itself could be useful or **reusable** for a number of scripting tasks, so we make it program neutral. Then, we have another script, but this one is dedicated to a single task: performing useless file system operations (IO). In this case, we would have two files:

1. `io_maker.sh` (which includes `library.sh` and uses `library.sh` functions)
2. `library.sh` (which contains declared functions, but does not execute them)

The `io_maker.sh` script simply imports or includes the `library.sh` script and inherits knowledge of any global variables, functions, and other inclusions. In this manner, `io_maker.sh` effectively thinks that these other available functions are its own and can execute them as if they were contained within it.

Including/importing a library script and using external functions

To prepare for this example, create the following two files and open both:

- `io_maker.sh`
- `library.sh`

Inside `library.sh`, add the following:

```
#!/bin/bash

function create_file() {
    local FNAME=$1
    touch "${FNAME}"
    ls "${FNAME}" # If output doesn't return a value - file is missing
}

function delete_file() {
    local FNAME=$1
    rm "${FNAME}"
    ls "${FNAME}" # If output doesn't return a value - file is missing
}
```

Inside `io_maker.sh`, add the following:

```
#!/bin/bash

source library.sh # You may need to include the path as it is relative
FNAME="my_test_file.txt"
create_file "${FNAME}"
delete_file "${FNAME}"

exit 0
```

When you run the script, you should get the same output:

```
$ bash io_maker.sh
my_test_file.txt
ls: cannot access 'my_test_file.txt': No such file or directory
```

Although not obvious, we can see that both functions are executed. The first line of output is the `ls` command, successfully finding `my_test_file.txt` after creating the file in `create_file()`. In the second line, we can see that ls returns an error when we delete the file passed in as a parameter.

Unfortunately, up until now, we have only been able to create and call functions, and execute commands. The next step, discussed in the next section, is to retrieve commands and function return codes or strings.

Retrieving return codes and output

Up until now, we have been using a command called `exit` intermittently to exit scripts. For those of you who are curious, you may have already scoured the web to find out what this command does, but the key concept to remember is that *every* script, command, or binary exits with a *return code*. Return codes are numeric and are limited to being between 0-255 because an unsigned 8-bit integer is used. If you use a value of −1, it will return `255`.

Okay, so return codes are useful in which ways? Return codes are useful when you want to know whether you found a match when performing a match (for example), and whether the command was completely successfully or there was an error. Let's dig into a real example using the `ls` command on the console:

```
$ ls ~/this.file.no.exist
ls: cannot access '/home/rbrash/this.file.no.exist': No such file or
directory
$ echo $?
2
$ ls ~/.bashrc
/home/rbrash/.bashrc
$ echo $?
0
```

Notice the return values? 0 or 2 in this example mean either success (0) or that there are errors (1 and 2). These are obtained by retrieving the $? variable and we could even set it to a variable like this:

```
$ ls ~/this.file.no.exist
ls: cannot access '/home/rbrash/this.file.no.exist': No such file or
directory
$ TEST=$?
$ echo $TEST
2
```

From this example, we now know what return codes are, and how we can use them to utilize results returned from functions, scripts, and commands.

Return code 101

Dig into your terminal and create the following Bash script:

```
#!/bin/bash
GLOBAL_RET=255

function my_function_global() {
    ls /home/${USER}/.bashrc
    GLOBAL_RET=$?
}
function my_function_return() {
    ls /home/${USER}/.bashrc
    return $?
}
function my_function_str() {
    local UNAME=$1
    local OUTPUT=""
    if [ -e /home/${UNAME}/.bashrc ]; then
        OUTPUT='FOUND IT'
    else
        OUTPUT='NOT FOUND'
    fi
    echo ${OUTPUT}
}

echo "Current ret: ${GLOBAL_RET}"
my_function_global "${USER}"
echo "Current ret after: ${GLOBAL_RET}"
GLOBAL_RET=255
echo "Current ret: ${GLOBAL_RET}"
my_function_return "${USER}"
```

```
GLOBAL_RET=$?
echo "Current ret after: ${GLOBAL_RET}"

# And for giggles, we can pass back output too!
GLOBAL_RET=""
echo "Current ret: ${GLOBAL_RET}"
GLOBAL_RET=$(my_function_str ${USER})
# You could also use GLOBAL_RET=`my_function_str ${USER}`
# Notice the back ticks "`"
echo "Current ret after: $GLOBAL_RET"
exit 0
```

The script will output the following before exiting with a return code of 0 (remember that ls returns 0 if run successfully):

```
rbrash@moon:~$ bash test.sh
Current ret: 255
/home/rbrash/.bashrc
Current ret after: 0
Current ret: 255
/home/rbrash/.bashrc
Current ret after: 0
Current ret:
Current ret after: FOUND IT
$
```

In this section, there are three functions that leverage three concepts:

1. `my_function_global` uses a `global` variable to return the command's return code
2. `my_function_return` uses the reserved word, `return`, and a value (the command's return code)
3. `my_function_str` uses a `fork` (a special operation) to execute a command and get the output (our string, which is echoed)

For option 3, there are several ways to get a string back from a function, including using the `eval` keyword. However, when using fork, it is best to be aware of the resources it may consume when running the same command many times just to get the output.

Linking commands, pipes, and input/output

This section is probably one of the most important in the book because it describes a fundamental and powerful feature on Linux and Unix: the ability to use pipes and redirect input or output. By themselves, pipes are a fairly trivial feature - commands and scripts can redirect their output to files or commands. So what? This could be considered a massive understatement in the Bash scripting world, because pipes and redirection allow you to enhance commands with the functionality of other commands or features.

Let's look into this with an example using commands called `tail` and `grep`. In this example, the user, Bob, wants to look at his logs in real time (live), but he only wants to find the entries related to the wireless interface. The name of Bob's wireless device can be found using the `iwconfig` command:

```
$ iwconfig
wlp3s0 IEEE 802.11abgn ESSID:"127.0.0.1-2.4ghz"
        Mode:Managed Frequency:2.412 GHz Access Point: 18:D6:C7:FA:26:B1
        Bit Rate=144.4 Mb/s Tx-Power=22 dBm
        Retry short limit:7 RTS thr:off Fragment thr:off
        Power Management:on
        Link Quality=58/70 Signal level=-52 dBm
        Rx invalid nwid:0 Rx invalid crypt:0 Rx invalid frag:0
        Tx excessive retries:0 Invalid misc:90 Missed beacon:0
```

The `iwconfig` command is deprecated now. The following commands also will give you wireless interface information:

```
$ iw dev               # This will give list of wireless interfaces
$ iw dev wlp3s0 link   # This will give detailed information about
particular wireless interface
```

Now that Bob knows his wireless card's identifying name (`wlp3s0`), Bob can search his system's logs. It is usually found within `/var/log/messages`. Using the `tail` command and the `-F` flag, which allows continuously outputting the logs to the console, Bob can now see *all* the logs for his system. Unfortunately, he would like to filter the logs using `grep`, such that only logs with the keyword `wlp3s0` are visible.

Bob is faced with a choice: does he search the file continuously, or can he combine `tail` and `grep` together to get the results he desires? The answer is yes—using *pipes*!

```
$ tail -F /var/log/messages | grep wlp3s0
Nov 10 11:57:13 moon kernel: wlp3s0: authenticate with 18:d6:c7:fa:26:b1
Nov 10 11:57:13 moon kernel: wlp3s0: send auth to 18:d6:c7:fa:26:b1 (try
1/3)
Nov 10 11:57:13 moon kernel: wlp3s0: send auth to 18:d6:c7:fa:26:b1 (try
2/3)
...
```

As new logs come in, Bob can now monitor them in real time and can stop the console output using *Ctrl+C*.

Using pipes, we can combine commands into powerful hybrid commands, extending the best features of each command into one single line. Remember pipes!

The usage and flexibility of pipes should be relatively straightforward, but what about directing the input and output of commands? This requires the introduction of three commands to get information from one place to another:

- `stdin` (standard in)
- `stdout` (standard out)
- `stderr` (standard error)

If we are thinking about a *single* program, `stdin` is anything that can be provided to it, usually either as a parameter or a user input, **using read** for example. `Stdout` and `stderr` are two **streams** where output can be sent. Usually, output for both is sent to the console for display, but what if you only want the errors within the `stderr` stream to go to a file?

```
$ ls /filethatdoesntexist.txt 2> err.txt
$ ls ~/ > stdout.txt
$ ls ~/ > everything.txt 2>&1 # Gets stderr and stdout
$ ls ~/ >> everything.txt 2>&1 # Gets stderr and stdout
$ cat err.txt
ls: cannot access '/filethatdoesntexist.txt': No such file or directory
$ cat stdout.txt
.... # A whole bunch of files in your home directory
```

When we `cat err.txt`, we can see the error output from the stderr stream. This is useful when you only want to record errors and not everything being output to the console. The key feature to observe from the snippet is the usage of **>, 2>,** and **2>&1**. With the arrows we can redirect the output to any file or even to other programs!

Take note of the difference between a single > and double >>. A single > **will truncate** any file that will have output directed to it, while >> **will append** any file.

There is a common error when redirecting both `stderr` and `stdout` to the same file. Bash should pick up the output to a file first, and then the duplication of the output file descriptors. For more information on file descriptors, see: https://en.wikipedia.org/wiki/File_descriptor

```
# This is correct
ls ~/ > everything.txt 2>&1
# This is erronous
ls ~/ 2>&1> everything.txt
```

Now that we know the basics of one of the most powerful features available in Bash, let's try an example—redirection and pipes bonzanza.

Redirection and pipe bonzanza

Open a shell and create a new bash file in your favorite editor:

```
#!/bin/sh

# Let's run a command and send all of the output to /dev/null
echo "No output?"
ls ~/fakefile.txt > /dev/null 2>&1

# Retrieve output from a piped command
echo "part 1"
HISTORY_TEXT=`cat ~/.bashrc | grep HIST`
echo "${HISTORY_TEXT}"

# Output the results to history.config
echo "part 2"
echo "${HISTORY_TEXT}" > "history.config"

# Re-direct history.config as input to the cat command
cat < history.config
```

```
# Append a string to history.config
echo "MY_VAR=1" >> history.config

echo "part 3 - using Tee"
# Neato.txt will contain the same information as the console
ls -la ~/fakefile.txt ~/ 2>&1 | tee neato.txt
```

First, `ls` is a way of producing an error and, instead of pushing erroneous output to the console, it is instead redirected to a special device in Linux called /dev/null. /dev/null is particularly useful as it is a dump for any input that will not be used again. Then, we combine the `cat` command with `grep` to find any lines of text with a pipe and use a fork to capture the output to a variable (HISTORY_TEXT).

Then, we echo the contents of HISTORY_TEXT to a file (history.config) using a stdout redirect. Using the history.configfile, we redirect cat to use the raw file—this will be displayed on the console.

Using a double >>, we append an arbitrary string to the history.config file.

Finally, we end the script with redirection for both stdout and stderr, a pipe,, and the tee command. The tee command is useful because it can be used to display content even if it has been redirected to a file (as we just demonstrated).

Getting program input parameters

Retrieving program input parameters or arguments is very similar to function parameters at the most basic level. They can be accessed in the same fashion as $1 (arg1), $2 (arg2), $3 (arg3), and so on. However, so far, we have seen a concept called **flags**, which allows you to perform neat things such as-l, --long-version, -v 10, --verbosity=10. **Flags** are effectively a user-friendly way to pass parameters or arguments to a program at runtime. For example:

```
bash myProgram.sh -v 99 --name=Ron -l Brash
```

Now that you know what flags are and how they can be helpful to improve your script, use the following section as a template.

Passing your program flags

After going into your shell and opening a new file in your favorite editor, let's get started by creating a Bash script that does the following:

- When no flags or arguments are specified, prints out a help message
- When either the -h or --help flags are set, it prints out a help message
- When the -f or --firstname flags are set, it sets the the first name variable
- When the -l or --lastname flags are set, it sets the the last name variable
- When *both* the firstname and lastname flags are set, it prints a welcome message and returns without error

In addition to the basic logic, we can see that the code leverages a piece of functionality called getopts. Getopts allows us to grab the program parameter flags for use within our program. There are also primitives, which we have learned as well—conditional logic, while loop, and case/switch statements. Once a script develops into more than a simple utility or provides more than a single function, the more basic Bash constructs will become commonplace.

```bash
#!/bin/bash

HELP_STR="usage: $0 [-h] [-f] [-l] [--firstname[=]<value>] [--lastname[=]<value] [--help]"

# Notice hidden variables and other built-in Bash functionality
optspec=":flh-:"
while getopts "$optspec" optchar; do
    case "${optchar}" in
        -)
            case "${OPTARG}" in
                firstname)
                    val="${!OPTIND}"; OPTIND=$(( $OPTIND + 1 ))
                    FIRSTNAME="${val}"
                    ;;
                lastname)
                    val="${!OPTIND}"; OPTIND=$(( $OPTIND + 1 ))
                        LASTNAME="${val}"
                    ;;
                help)
                    val="${!OPTIND}"; OPTIND=$(( $OPTIND + 1 ))
                    ;;
                *)
                    if [ "$OPTERR" = 1 ] && [ "${optspec:0:1}" != ":" ];
then
                        echo "Found an unknown option --${OPTARG}" >&2
```

```
            fi
            ;;
        esac;;
    f)
            val="${!OPTIND}"; OPTIND=$(( $OPTIND + 1 ))
            FIRSTNAME="${val}"
            ;;
    l)
            val="${!OPTIND}"; OPTIND=$(( $OPTIND + 1 ))
            LASTNAME="${val}"
            ;;
    h)
        echo "${HELP_STR}" >&2
        exit 2
        ;;
    *)
        if [ "$OPTERR" != 1 ] || [ "${optspec:0:1}" = ":" ]; then
            echo "Error parsing short flag: '-${OPTARG}'" >&2
            exit 1
        fi

        ;;
    esac
done

# Do we have even one argument?
if [ -z "$1" ]; then
  echo "${HELP_STR}" >&2
  exit 2
fi

# Sanity check for both Firstname and Lastname
if [ -z "${FIRSTNAME}" ] || [ -z "${LASTNAME}" ]; then
  echo "Both firstname and lastname are required!"
  exit 3
fi

echo "Welcome ${FIRSTNAME} ${LASTNAME}!"

exit 0
```

When we execute the preceding program, we should expect responses similar to the following:

```
$ bash flags.sh
usage: flags.sh [-h] [-f] [-l] [--firstname[=]<value>] [--
lastname[=]<value] [--help]
$ bash flags.sh -h
```

```
usage: flags.sh [-h] [-f] [-l] [--firstname[=]<value>] [--
lastname[=]<value] [--help]
$ bash flags.sh --fname Bob
Both firstname and lastname are required!
rbrash@moon:~$ bash flags.sh --firstname To -l Mater
Welcome To Mater!
```

Getting additional information about commands

As we progress, you may see this book use many commands extensively and without exhaustive explanations. Without polluting this entire book with an introduction to Linux and useful commands, there are a couple of commands available that are really handy: man and info.

The man command, or manual command, is quite extensive and even has multiple sections when the same entry exists in different categories. For the purposes of investigating executable programs or shell commands, category 1 is sufficient. Let's look at the entry for the mount command:

```
$ man mount
...
MOUNT(8) System Administration MOUNT(8)
NAME
 mount - mount a filesystem
SYNOPSIS
 mount [-l|-h|-V]
 mount -a [-fFnrsvw] [-t fstype] [-O optlist]
 mount [-fnrsvw] [-o options] device|dir
 mount [-fnrsvw] [-t fstype] [-o options] device dir
DESCRIPTION
 All files accessible in a Unix system are arranged in one big tree, the
 file hierarchy, rooted at /. These files can be spread out over sev-
 eral devices. The mount command serves to attach the filesystem found
 on some device to the big file tree. Conversely, the umount(8) command
 will detach it again.
...
(Press 'q' to Quit)
$
```

Alternatively, there is the `info` command, which will give you information should info pages exist for the item you are looking for.

 Getting used to the style of the man and info pages can easily save you time by allowing you to access information quickly, especially if you don't have the internet.

Summary

In this chapter, we introduced the concept of variables, types, and assignments. We also covered some basic Bash programming primitives for for loops, while, and switch statements. Later on, we learned what functions are, how they are used, and how to pass parameters.

In the next chapter, we will learn about several bolt-on technologies to make Bash even more extensive.

2
Acting Like a Typewriter and File Explorer

In this chapter, we will introduce the following:

- Basic searching for strings and files
- Using wildcards and regexes
- Math and calculations in script
- Striping/altering/sorting/deleting/searching strings with Bash only
- Using SED and AWK to remove/replace substrings
- Formatting your data/output using echo and printf
- Readying your script for different languages with internationalization
- Calculating statistics and reducing duplicates based on file contents
- Using file attributes with conditional logic
- Reading delimited data and altered output format

Introduction

Hopefully, the previous Bash crash course chapter provided more than a hint of the utility and power of Bash. On the other hand, this chapter introduces several *bolt-on* technologies to make Bash even more extensive when searching for items and text, or automating file explorer/file system operations.

By itself, Bash is merely a powerful scripting language, but much of Bash's flexibility comes from being able to "glue" other technologies (tools or languages) together to make the output more useful. In other words, Bash is a base platform similar to how some auto/car lovers choose a particular platform before making their modifications. Will a modified car do everything, even with enhancements? Certainly not, but it can make it more powerful or useful in specific cases, and at least provides four wheels for movement.

Not only do common scripts contain a series of commands for automation, they often include **logic** to modify strings such as the following:

- Removing trailing characters
- Replacing sections of words (substrings)
- Searching for strings in files
- Finding files
- Testing file types (directory, file, empty, and so on)
- Performing small calculations
- Limiting the scope of searches or data (filtering)
- Modifying the contents of variables (strings inside of string variables)

This logic that modifies, limits, and even replaces input/output data can be very powerful when you need to execute broad searches for a specific string or when you have copious amounts of data. Terminals chock; full of output or massive data files can be very daunting to explore!

However, there is one very important concept that still needs to be discussed, and that is **recursive** functionality. Recursive functionality can apply to script functions, logic, and even a command operation. For example, you can use **grep** to **recursively** crawl an entire directory until no more files remain, or you can recursively execute a function inside of itself until a condition is met (for example, printing a single character at a time within a string):

```
# e.g. File system
# / (start here)
# /home (oh we found home)
# /home/user (neat there is a directory inside it called user)
# /home/user/.. (even better, user has files - lets look in them too)
# /etc/ # We are done with /home and its "children" so lets look in /etc
# ... # Until we are done
```

 Be careful with recursion (especially with functions), as it can sometimes be really slow depending on the complexity of the structure (for example, file system or size of files). Also if there is a logic error, you can keep executing functions recursively forever!

This chapter is all about limiting data, utilizing it, modifying it, internationalizing it, replacing it, and even searching for it in the first place.

Basic searching for strings and files

Imagine searching for a four leaf clover in a big garden. It would be really hard (and it is still really hard for computers). Thankfully, words are not images and text on a computer is easily searchable depending on the format. The term **format** has to be used because if your tool cannot understand a given type of text (**encoding**), then you might have trouble recognizing a **pattern** or even detecting that there is text at all!

Typically, when you are looking at the console, text files, source code (C, C++, Bash, HTML), spreadsheets, XML, and other types, you are looking at it in **ASCII** or **UTF**. ASCII is a commonly used format in the `*NIX` world on the console. There is also the UTF **encoding scheme**, which is an improvement upon ASCII and can support a variety of extended characters that were not present in computing originally. It comes in a number of formats such as UTF-8, UTF-16, and UTF32.

 When you hear the words encoding and decoding, it is similar to encryption and decryption. The purpose is not to hide something, but rather to transform some data into something appropriate for the use case. For example, transmission, usage with languages, and compression. ASCII and UTF are not the only types your target data might be in. In various types of files, you may encounter different types of encoding of data. This is a different problem that's specific to your data and will need additional considerations.

In this recipe, we will begin the process of searching for strings and a couple of ways to search for some of your own needles in a massive haystack of data. Let's dig in.

Getting ready

Besides having a terminal open (and your favorite text editor, if necessary), we only need a couple of core commands such as `grep`, `ls`, `mkdir`, `touch`, `traceroute`, `strings`, `wget`, `xargs`, and `find`.

Assuming that your user already has the correct permissions for your usage (and authorized, of course), we will need to generate data to begin searching:

```
$ ~/
$ wget --recursive --no-parent https://www.packtpub.com www.packtpub.com #
Takes awhile
$ traceroute packtpub.com > traceroute.txt
$ mkdir -p www.packtpub.com/filedir www.packtpub.com/emptydir
$ touch www.packtpub.com/filedir/empty.txt
```

```
$ touch www.packtpub.com/findme.xml; echo "<xml>"
www.packtpub.com/findme.xml
```

How to do it...

Using the data obtained by recursively **crawling** the Packt Publishing website, we can see that inside of **www.packtpub.com** the entire website is available. Wow! We also created some test data directories and files.

1. Next, open up a terminal and create the following script:

```bash
#!/bin/bash

# Let's find all the files with the string "Packt"
DIRECTORY="www.packtpub.com/"
SEARCH_TERM="Packt"

# Can we use grep?
grep "${SEARCH_TERM}" ~/* > result1.txt 2&> /dev/null

# Recursive check
grep -r "${SEARCH_TERM}" "${DIRECTORY}" > result2.txt

# What if we want to check for multiple terms?
grep -r -e "${SEARCH_TERM}" -e "Publishing" "${DIRECTORY}" >
result3.txt

# What about find?
find "${DIRECTORY}" -type f -print | xargs grep "${SEARCH_TERM}" >
result4.txt

# What about find and looking for the string inside of a specific
type of content?
find "${DIRECTORY}" -type f -name "*.xml" ! -name "*.css" -print |
xargs grep "${SEARCH_TERM}" > result5.txt

# Can this also be achieved with wildcards and subshell?
grep "${SEARCH_TERM}" $(ls -R "${DIRECTORY}"*.{html,txt}) >
result6.txt
RES=$?

if [ ${RES} -eq 0 ]; then
  echo "We found results!"
else
  echo "It broke - it shouldn't happen (Packt is everywhere)!"
fi
```

```
# Or for bonus points - a personal favorite
history | grep "ls" # This is really handy to find commands you ran
yesterday!

# Aaaannnd the lesson is:
echo "We can do a lot with grep!"
exit 0
```

 Notice in the script the use of ~/* ?. This refers to our home directory and introduces the * wildcard, which allows us to specify anything from that point on. There will be more on the concept of wildcards and regexes later in this chapter.

2. If you remain in your home directory (~/) and run the script, the output should be similar to the following:

```
$ bash search.sh; ls -lah result*.txt
We found results!
We can do a lot with grep!
-rw-rw-r-- 1 rbrash rbrash 0 Nov 14 14:33 result1.txt
-rw-rw-r-- 1 rbrash rbrash 1.2M Nov 14 14:33 result2.txt
-rw-rw-r-- 1 rbrash rbrash 1.2M Nov 14 14:33 result3.txt
-rw-rw-r-- 1 rbrash rbrash 1.2M Nov 14 14:33 result4.txt
-rw-rw-r-- 1 rbrash rbrash 33 Nov 14 14:33 result5.txt
-rw-rw-r-- 1 rbrash rbrash 14K Nov 14 14:33 result6.txt
```

How it works...

This section is a bit of a *doozy* because we are leading up to another more expansive topic, which is using regexes and wildcards with strings. We introduced them, but also showed you that you can search for terms with ${SEARCH_TERM} or *Packt* specifically without their use—it's just more work and more statements. Can you imagine writing a specific grep statement for each term such as Packt1, Packt2, Packt3, and onwards? No fun.

Using the Packt Publishing website as a *baseline* data set, we *grepped* our way through the directory using the grep command, targeting only our current location, our user's home directory. **Grep** is a powerful tool that can be used to parse the output of commands and files using patterns, regexs, and user supplied parameters. In this case, we did not expect any string to be found matching *Packt* because **www.packtpub.com** is *not* the same as **www.Packtpub.com**. Therefore, result1.txt is an empty file.

Grep and many other utilities can be case-sensitive. To use `grep` in a way that's case insensitive, use the `-i` flag.

In the second use of `grep`, we used the recursive flag (`-r`) and found many matches. By default, `grep` returns the path (containing the filename) of a match, and the line the match occurred within. To find the line number, you can also use the flag (`-n`).

In the third example, we demonstrated that `grep` can be used with multiple user-supplied arguments:

```
$ grep -e "Packt" -e "Publishing" -r ~/www.packtpub.com/
```

In this recipe, we are searching using a *brute-force* mechanism, which means we'll find it all by using all of our strength, literally. When performing searching on large amounts of data, or even when you perform something as seemingly simple as a search on the `PacktPublishing` website, more advanced and targeted algorithms help you find exactly what you want more efficiently and quicker than what we are doing here!

In the fourth and fifth executed examples, we use the `find` command. We also pair it with pipes and the `xargs` command as well. By itself, `find` is another very powerful CLI utility that can be used to perform search functionality (and consequently, damaging things if used irresponsibly/maliciously):

```
$ find "${DIRECTORY}" -type f -print | xargs grep "${SEARCH_TERM}" >
result4.txt
```

In the preceding `find` command, we are using `-type f`, which means that we are looking for files only within `${DIRECTORY}`. Then, we pipe the results into the `xargs` command for use with grep. Wait! What is xargs!? `Xargs` is a command that's commonly used in tandem with a pipe to pass newline (carriage return) data to another command. For example, if we run ls `-l` (with the long flag), the results are returned like this (we've added the invisible line break or \n to illustrate this):

```
$ ls -l
drwxr-xr-x 7 rbrash rbrash 4096 Nov 13 21:48 Desktop\n
drwxr-xr-x 2 rbrash rbrash 4096 Feb 11 2017 Documents\n
drwxr-xr-x 7 rbrash rbrash 32768 Nov 14 10:54 Downloads\n
-rw-r--r-- 1 rbrash rbrash 8980 Feb 11 2017 examples.desktop\n
...
```

If we piped the results directly into another command that expected an input like the following, it would break!

```
$ someProgram Desktop\n Documents\n Downloads\n ...
```

Instead, `someProgram` requires input values separated by a space and *not* new lines:

```
$ someProgram Desktop Documents Downloads ...
```

This is why you use `xargs`: to remove or convert the new lines into something less problematic.

Going back to the second `find` command example, you can see that we used the `-name` and `! -name` parameters. `-name` is simple; we are looking for a file with a specific user-supplied name. In the second `! -name` instance, the `!` means without or *not* with that name. This is called **inverted logic**.

We also used the `*` wildcard again in a different context than in the first example using `grep` (again, more on this later). Instead, this time, we used the `*` to match anything before the file's extension (`*.xml` or `*.css`). It can even be used like this:

```
$ ls -l /etc/*/*.txt
-rw-r--r-- 1 root root 17394 Nov 10 2015 /etc/X11/rgb.txt
```

In the following `grep` command, we use an inline subshell execution of the `ls` command using wildcards. Then, we take the result by setting `${RES}` to `$?`. `$?` is a special variable used to get the return code. Using the value within `${RES}`, we can now provide a bit of conditional logic if results are found and appropriately `echo`:

```
We found results!
```

Right before we exited the shell, we thought we would throw in a bonus: you can search your past ran commands using the `history` command and `grep`.

Using wildcards and regexes

As we saw in the previous section, there was this new concept of recursive functions and the introduction of wildcards. This section will extend upon those same fundamental primitives to create more advanced searches using regexes and globbing.

It will also extend them with a number of built-in Bash features, and some one-liners (nifty tricks) to enhance our searches. In short:

- A wildcard can be: *, {*.ooh,*.ahh}, /home/*/path/*.txt, [0-10], [!a], ?, [a,p] m
- A regex can be: $, ^, *, [], [!], | (be careful to escape this)

Globbing basically refers to a far more computer-eccentric term, which can be simply described in layman terms as **extended pattern matching**. Wildcards are the **symbols** used to describe patterns, and **regex** is short for **regular expression**, which are terms used to describe the pattern that is to match a series of data.

 Globbing in Bash is powerful, but likely not the best place to perform even more advanced or intricate pattern matching. In these cases, Python or another language/tool might be more appropriate.

As we can imagine, globbing and pattern matching are really useful, but they cannot be used by every utility or application. Usually, though, they can be used at the command line with utilities such as grep. For example:

```
$ ls -l | grep '[[:lower:]][[:digit:]]' # Notice no result
$ touch z0.test
$ touch a1.test
$ touch A2.test
$ ls -l | grep '[[:lower:]][[:digit:]]'
-rw-rw-r-- 1 rbrash rbrash 0 Nov 15 11:31 z0.test
-rw-rw-r-- 1 rbrash rbrash 0 Nov 15 11:31 a1.test
```

Using the ls command, which is piped into grep with a regex, we can see that after we touch three files and re-run the command that the regex allowed us to correctly filter the output for files starting with a lowercase character, which are followed by a single digit.

If we wanted to further enhance grep (or another command), we could use any of the following:

- [:alpha:]: Alphabetic (case-insensitive)
- [:lower:]: Lowercase printable characters
- [:upper:]: Uppercase printable characters
- [:digit:]: Numbers in decimal 0 to 9
- [:alnum:]: Alphanumeric (all digits and alphabetic characters)
- [:space:]: White space meaning spaces, tabs, and newlines

- [:graph:]: Printable characters excluding spaces
- [:print:]: Printable characters including spaces
- [:punct:]: Punctuation (for example, a period)
- [:cntrl:]: Control characters (non-printable characters like when a signal is generated when you use *Ctrl + C)*
- [:xdigit:]: Hexadecimal characters

Getting ready

Besides having a terminal open (and your favorite text editor, if necessary), we only need a couple of core commands: grep, tr, cut, and touch. We're assuming that the www.packtpub.com directory that we crawled through in the previous step is still available:

```
$ cd ~/
$ touch {a..c}.test
$ touch {A..C}[0..2].test2
$ touch Z9.test3 Z9\,test2 Z9..test2
$ touch ~/Desktop/Test.pdf
```

How to do it...

Let's get started:

1. Open a terminal, and an editor of your choice to create a new script.
2. Inside of your script, add the following:

```
#!/bin/bash
STR1='123 is a number, ABC is alphabetic & aBC123 is alphanumeric.'

echo "-----------------------------------------------"
# Want to find all of the files beginning with an uppercase
character and end with .pdf?
ls * | grep [[:upper:]]*.pdf

echo "-----------------------------------------------"
# Just all of the directories in your current directory?
ls -l [[:upper:]]*

echo "-----------------------------------------------"
# How about all of the files we created with an expansion using the
{ } brackets?
```

```
ls [:lower:].test .

echo "----------------------------------------------------"
# Files with a specific extension OR two?
echo ${STR1} > test.txt
ls *.{test,txt}

echo "----------------------------------------------------"
# How about looking for specific punctuation and output on the same
line
echo "${STR1}" | grep -o [[:punct:]] | xargs echo

echo "----------------------------------------------------"
# How about using groups and single character wildcards (only 5
results)
ls | grep -E "([[:upper:]])([[:digit:]])?.test?" | tail -n 5

exit 0
```

3. Now, execute the script and your console should be flooded with the output. Most importantly, let's look at the last five results. Notice the Z9(,) and Z9.test(3) among the results? This is the power of a regex at work! Okay, so we get that we can now create and search for a bunch of folders or files using variables, but can I use regexes to find things like variable parameters? Absolutely! See the next step.

4. In the console, try the following:

```
$ grep -oP 'name="\K.*?(?=")' www.packtpub.com/index.html
```

5. Again, in the console, try the following:

```
$ grep -P 'name=' www.packtpub.com/index.html
```

6. Can we do better using commands like tr to remove new lines when finding instances of IF that may span multiple lines?

```
$ tr '\n' ' ' < www.packtpub.com/index.html | grep -o
'<title>.*</title>'
```

7. Now, let's remove a bit more gunk from the screen using cut as a finale. Usually, the console is 80 characters wide, so let's add a line number and trim the output from grep:

```
$ grep -nP 'name=' www.packtpub.com/index.html | cut -c -80
```

Entire books have been dedicated to parsing data with regexes, but the key thing to note is that regexes are not always the best option for either performance or for markup languages like HTML. For example, when parsing HTML, it is best to use a parser that is aware of the language itself and any language-specific nuances.

How it works...

As you may have guessed, snooping through lots of data without regexes and wildcards can be a nightmare for the uninitiated. An even scarier one might even occur when your expressions don't use the correct terms or a valid (and accurate) expression to begin with. However, wildcards are quite useful on the command line when trying to **craft** strings together, find data quickly, and finding files. Sometimes, it the usability of the search result that's irrelevant if I'm merely looking to find the filename and rough location/line of a specific occurrence. For example, where is this CSS class in what file?

Well, you made it through the script and ran several commands to get a real-world idea of how to use regexes and wildcards at a surface level. Let's turn back the clock and walk through the recipe.

In step 1, we opened a console, created a simple script, and executed it. The output results were then displayed on the console:

```
$ bash test.sh
------------------------------------------------
Linux-Journal-2017-08.pdf
Linux-Journal-2017-09.pdf
Linux-Journal-2017-10.pdf
Test.pdf
------------------------------------------------
-rw-rw-r-- 1 rbrash rbrash 0 Nov 15 22:13 A0.test2
-rw-rw-r-- 1 rbrash rbrash 0 Nov 15 22:13 A1.test2
-rw-rw-r-- 1 rbrash rbrash 0 Nov 15 22:13 A2.test2
-rw-rw-r-- 1 rbrash rbrash 0 Nov 15 22:13 B0.test2
-rw-rw-r-- 1 rbrash rbrash 0 Nov 15 22:13 B1.test2
-rw-rw-r-- 1 rbrash rbrash 0 Nov 15 22:13 B2.test2
-rw-rw-r-- 1 rbrash rbrash 0 Nov 15 22:13 C0.test2
-rw-rw-r-- 1 rbrash rbrash 0 Nov 15 22:13 C1.test2
-rw-rw-r-- 1 rbrash rbrash 0 Nov 15 22:13 C2.test2
-rw-rw-r-- 1 rbrash rbrash 0 Nov 15 22:13 Z9,test2
-rw-rw-r-- 1 rbrash rbrash 0 Nov 15 22:13 Z9..test2
-rw-rw-r-- 1 rbrash rbrash 0 Nov 15 22:13 Z9.test3

Desktop:
```

```
total 20428
drwxrwxr-x 2 rbrash rbrash 4096 Nov 15 12:55 book
# Lots of files here too

Documents:
total 0

Downloads:
total 552776
-rw------- 1 root root 1024 Feb 11 2017 ~
... # I have a lot of files for this book

Music:
total 0

Pictures:
total 2056
drwxrwxr-x 2 rbrash rbrash 4096 Sep 6 21:56 backgrounds

Public:
total 0

Templates:
total 0

Videos:
total 4
drwxrwxr-x 13 rbrash rbrash 4096 Aug 11 10:42 movies
------------------------------------------------
a.test b.test c.test
------------------------------------------------
a.test b.test c.test test.txt
------------------------------------------------
, & .
------------------------------------------------
C0.test2
C1.test2
C2.test2
Z9,test2
Z9.test3
```

It could be a lot scarier! Right? In the first line, we begin by chasing down some PDFs that start with a capital (uppercase) letter. The line `ls * | grep [[:upper:]]*.pdf` uses the `ls` command with a `*` wildcard (for everything) and then pipes the output into `grep` with a simple regex. The regex is `[[:upper:]]` followed by another `*` wildcard to combine the `.pdf` string. This produces our search results, which at a minimum will contain `Test.pdf` (my results returned PDFs for a popular Linux journal too!).

Then, we perform almost the same search using `ls -l [[:upper:]]*` , but using the `ls` directory with a regex will return a large amount of data (if all of the folders have contents). It begins in the current directory where the script is located, and then marches one directory deep and prints the contents. A neat feature is the use of the `-l` flag, which will produce *long* results and print the size of the directory in bytes.

Next, we use `ls` and look for all files beginning with a lowercase character and end with the `.test` extension. Little did you know, when you set up this recipe, you also saw wildcards and an expansion at work: `touch {a..c}.test` . The `touch` command created three files: `a.test`, `b.test`, and `c.test`. The `ls` command with this simple regex returns the names of the previous three files.

Again, we use the `ls` command with the (`*`), wildcard and expansion brackets to match for file extensions: `ls *.{test,txt}`. It searches for files with any name (`*`), which are then concatenated with a period (`.`), followed by either `test` or `txt` extensions.

Next, in step 7, we combined a few things we have learned using pipes, `grep`, `xargs`, and a regex in the command: `echo "${STR1}" | grep -o [[:punct:]] | xargs echo`. The fact that the output from grep will be in `\n` delimited form (new lines for each instance found), this will break our intention to have all of the values echoed to the console in this form and thereby we need `xargs` to fix the output into parameters `echo` can properly use. For example, `echo "item1\n item2\n item3\n"` will not work, but with `xargs`, it will look like: `echo "item1"  "item2" "item3"`.

And in the final command, we finally arrive at a *crazier* regex, which in truth is actually quite tame: `ls | grep -E "([[:upper:]])([[:digit:]])?.test?." | tail -n 5`. It introduces a couple of concepts, including groups (the parentheses), (?) wildcards, and how you can combine multiple expression components, and `tail`.

Using `grep`, the `-E` (expression flag), and two groups (the expressions inside of the parenthesis), we can combine them with the `?` regex operator. This acts as a wildcard for a single character:

```
C0.test2
C1.test2
C2.test2
Z9,test2
Z9.test3
```

We can see that the last five results were returned, starting with a capital letter, followed by a number, a character (either . or ,), and then the word test and a number. We created one test file called Z9..test2. Notice how it was not included among the list items? This was because we did not use an expression like this:

```
$ ls | grep -E "([[:upper:]])([[:digit:]])?.?.test?"
```

In step 4, we run a particular regex using grep and -oP flags, grep -oP 'name="\K.*?(?=")' www.packtpub.com/index.html, on top of our recently crawled archive of www.packtpub.com. The -o flag means output only matching values, and -P is for using the Perl expressions.

Notice all of the values contained with double quotes? It's looking for *any* match that matches the pattern name="anythingGoesHere". It's certainly not extremely useful by itself, but it illustrates the point of being able to quickly get values (for example, what if the name was very specific? You could alter name= to another value and get the exact same result!).

Following along the same context, in step 5, we can also find *all* occurrences of name=: grep -P 'name=' www.packtpub.com/index.html. This type of command is useful for understanding the context of information or merely the existence of it; this comes back to the idea of looking for values in CSS, C/C++, and other data/source files.

Onward to step 6, we are looking for the title HTML tag. Normally, you should use a dedicated HTML parser, but if we wanted to use grep with regexes in a hurry—we can! The tr '\n' ' ' < www.packtpub.com/index.html | grep -o '<title>.*</title>' command uses the translate function (tr) to convert the \n or newline special character into an empty space. This is useful when data has a markup that may span multiple lines.

In our closing step, we end with a bit of fine-tuning when performing broad searches. We simply use grep to provide us with the line number and filename. Using cut, we an trim the remaining characters of the output on the console (this can be really useful):

```
$ grep -nHP 'name=' www.packtpub.com/index.html | cut -c -80
```

 Regexes can also be tested online using a number of regex simulators! One popular and free tool available online is: https://regexr.com/.

Don't forget that some regex functionalities also allow you to nest commands within groups! We didn't demonstrate this functionality, but it exists with acceptable results in some use cases!

Math and calculations in script

After a grueling introduction to the world of wildcards and regexes for searches, we're going to move on to being able to perform some basic mathematical operations at the console. If you haven't already tried, what happens when you run something like the following in the Bash shell? Does it look like this?

```
$ 1*5
1*5: command not found
```

Command not found? Certainly, we know the computer can do *math*, but clearly Bash is unable to interpret mathematical operations in this way. We have to ensure that Bash is able to **interpret** these operations correctly through the use of:

- The expr command (antiquated)
- The bc command
- POSIX Bash shell expansion
- Another language/program to do the *dirty* work

Let's try again, but using the POSIX Bash shell expansion:

```
$ echo $((1*5))
5
```

We got the expected answer of 5, but where does this go wrong? It goes wrong when using division and floats because Bash works primarily with integers:

```
$ echo $((1/5))
0
```

True, 1 divided by 5 is 0, but there is a remainder missing! And this is why we may rely on other methods to perform simple mathematics.

One of the many uses or reasons to use equations and `math` in a script is to determine sizes of file system partitions. Can you imagine what may happen if a disk becomes too full? Or that we may want to automatically archive a directory if it reaches a predetermined size? Of course, this is theoretical, but things can and do break if we let a file system silently become full!

The following recipe is about determining the size of a tarball (and contents), the remaining available space on the destination partition, and whether the operation could continue or be canceled.

Getting ready

This recipe is going to take into account a few interesting things:

- Bash can't do everything well
- Other utilities exist (for example, `bc`)
- We can create our own in another language like C
- Creating a tarball

 Sometimes, on small embedded systems, Python might not be available, but Bash (or a close relative) and C are. This is where being able to perform math without extra programs (that may not be available) can come in handy!

We will use the following command to make sure that we have all of the utilities installed for this experiment:

```
$ sudo apt-get install -y bc tar
```

Now, we need to create a tarball called `archive.tar.gz`:

```
$ dd if=/dev/zero of=empty.bin bs=1k count=10000
$ tar -zcvf archive.tar.gz empty.bin
$ rm empty.bin
```

We realize that the purpose of creating/compiling a simple program that is not written in Bash may be beyond the scope of this book, but it can be a helpful skill. To do this, we will need to install GCC, which is short for the GNU Compiler Collection. This sounds terribly complex and we assure you that we did all the hard work:

```
$ sudo apt-get install -y gcc
```

The preceding command installs the compiler, and now we need the C source code (in order to compile a *simple* C program). Open up a console and retrieve the code using:

```
$ wget
https://raw.githubusercontent.com/PacktPublishing/Bash-Cookbook/master/chap
ter%2002/mhelper.c
```

This code is also available on Github at `https://github.com/`
`PacktPublishing/Bash-Cookbook`.

To compile the code, we will use `gcc` and `-lm` (this refers to `libmath`) as follows:

```
$ gcc -Wall -02 -o mhelper main.c -lmath
```

If the compiler completes successfully (which it should), you will be left with a utility binary called `mhelper` (or math helper). We can also add this to our list of local commands by copying it to `/bin` using `sudo` and `cp`:

```
$ sudo cp mhelper /bin; sudo chmod a+x /bin/mhelper;
```

Now, `mhelper` can be used for basic operations such as division, multiplication, addition, and subtraction:

```
$ mhelper "var1" "-" "var2"
```

The `mhelper` code is not designed to be particularly robust and to handle specific edge cases, but rather to demonstrate that another utility can be used. Python and numpy would be an excellent alternatives!

How to do it...

Using the `mhelper` binary, `bc`, and other expressions, we can begin the recipe:

1. Begin by opening a terminal and an editor to create a new script called `mathexp.sh` with the following contents:

```
#!/bin/bash
# Retrieve file system information and remove header
TARBALL="archive.tar.gz"
CURRENT_PART_ALL=$(df --output=size,avail,used /home -B 1M | tail -
n1)
```

```
# Iterate through and fill array
IFS=' ' read -r -a array <<< $CURRENT_PART_ALL

# Retrieve the size of the contents of the tarball
COMPRESSED_SZ=$(tar tzvf "${TARBALL}" | sed 's/ \+/ /g' | cut -f3 -
d' ' | sed '2,$s/^/+ /' | paste -sd' ' | bc)

echo "First inspection - is there enough space?"
if [ ${array[1]} -lt ${COMPRESSED_SZ} ]; then
    echo "There is not enough space to decompress the binary"
    exit 1
else
  echo "Seems we have enough space on first inspection -
continuing"
  VAR=$((${array[0]} - ${array[2]}))
  echo "Space left: ${VAR}"
fi

echo "Safety check - do we have at least double the space?"
CHECK=$((${array[1]}*2))
echo "Double - good question? $CHECK"

# Notice the use of the bc command?
RES=$(echo "$(mhelper "${array[1]}" "/" "2")>0" | bc -l)
if [[ "${RES}" == "1" ]]; then
  echo "Spppppaaaaccee (imagine zombies)"
fi

# We know that this will break! (Bash is driven by integers)
# if [ $(mhelper "${array[2]}" "/" "2") -gt 0 ]; then
  #~ echo "Spppppaaaaccee (imagine zombies) - syntax error"
# fi
# What if we tried this with Bash and a concept again referring to
floats
# e.g., 0.5
# It would break
# if [ $((${array[2]} * 0.5 )) -gt 0 ]; then
  # echo "Spppppaaaaccee (imagine zombies) - syntax error"
# fi

# Then untar
tar xzvf ${TARBALL}
RES=$?
if [ ${RES} -ne 0 ]; then
  echo "Error decompressing the tarball!"
  exit 1
fi
```

```
echo "Decompressing tarball complete!"
exit 0
```

2. Now, running the script should produce an output similar to the following:

```
First inspection - is there enough space?
Seems we have enough space on first inspection - continuing
Space left: 264559
Safety check - do we have at least double the space?
Double - good question ? 378458
Spppppaaaaccee (imagine zombies)
empty.bin
Decompressing tarball complete!
```

Great! So we can use Bash size calculations, the `bc` command, and our binary. If you want to calculate the radius of a circle (which will certainly get you a float value) or a percentage, for example, you will need to be aware of this limitation in Bash.

To bring this recipe to a close, it is important to note that the `expr` command still exists, but it is deprecated. Using `$(( your equation ))` is recommended as the preferred method in new scripts.

Using the same premise using the `mhelper` binary or `$((..))` scripting, you can also calculate percentages for situations that need variable output (for example, not whole numbers). For example, calculating screen sizes based on percentages while a whole number will be desired, you can then round up or down post calculation.

How it works...

First things first, as this recipe alluded to—we noticed that the Bash shell doesn't like decimal numbers with fractions or even non-whole numbers. Wait, math!? Unfortunately, we can't hide all the details, but in programming, there are a couple of concepts that you should be aware of:

- Signed and unsigned numbers
- Floats, doubles, and integers

The first concept is fairly simple—current computers are binary, which means they compute using zeros (0) and ones (1). This means that they work in powers of 2^. Without getting into a lesson about basic computer science, if you see a value (datatype) that is an int (integer) and that it is a 32 bit number, this means that the maximum value if it begins at 0 is 4,294,967,295 in decimal (2^32). This makes one critical assumption and that is that all numbers (0 included) are positive. This positive or negative property is called **sign**! If a datatype mentions signed or unsigned—now you know what it means!

However, there is a consequence of whether something is signed and that is that the maximum positive or negative value is decreased because one bit is used to represent sign. A signed 32 bit int (which can also be referred to as int32) shall now have a range of (−)2,147,483,647 to (+)2,147,483,647.

 As a note from the author, I realize that some of the computer science definitions are not computer science correct, meaning that I tweaked some of their meanings to make sure the key points got across in *most* general situations.

On another note, Bash only uses integers and you may have already seen that when you divide a value like 1/5, the answer is 0. True, it is not divisible, but the answer is 0.20 as a fraction. We also cannot multiply numbers that have a decimal point as well! Therefore, we have to use other programs such as bc or mhelper.

If you are keen on computers, you also know that there are floats, doubles, and other datatypes to represent numbers. Mhelper and bc can help you deal with these types of numbers when the concept of integers fails (for example, resulting numbers are not whole numbers when dividing).

1. Back to the recipe, and in step 1:
   - We created a script that will check the /home directory to determine how much size is available using the df command. Using tail, another command that can be used to reduce output, we skip the first line of output and pipe all output into the $CURRENT_PART_ALL variable (or all current partition information).
   - Then, the contents of the $CURRENT_PART_ALL variable are read into an array using the read command. Notice the use of the re-direction errors: <<<. This is called a **here-string**, which in simple terms expands the variable and feeds it into stdin.

- Now, the /home partitions storage information is inside of an array, and we have a tarball (or a file that compresses and contains the contents within), where we need to know the size of the contents within the tarball. To do this, we use a long-winded command with multiple piped commands, which retrieves the size of the contained elements and pushes them through the bc command.

- Upon determining the size of the elements contained within our archive, we validate the calculated size against the remaining available space. This value is inside of the array element[1]. If the available space is less than equal to the extracted files, then exit. Otherwise, print the remaining size after performing.

- For fun, we combined forking a subshell to retrieve the division results of the mhelper, which are piped through bc. This is so we can determine if there is enough space as a mere boolean value of true (1) or false (0).

- Since we assume we have enough space, we untar (decompress and extract the contents) the $TARBALL. If the tar command returns a value not equal to 0, then exit with an error. Otherwise, exit with success.

2. After executing our script, the contents of the tarball (empty.bin) should be present in the current working directory.

Inside of the script, we put two different evaluations in the comments, which would return floating point values or errors in syntax. We included them for your awareness and to drive the main lesson home.
Did we miss anything? Absolutely! We never checked the size of the tarball itself and made sure that its size was among the used space when performing a check to determine the remaining free space. One should always be careful when performing and enforcing size restrictions!

Striping/altering/sorting/deleting/searching strings with Bash only

So far, we have seen inkling of the power of commands available in Linux, and some of these are among the most powerful: sed and grep. However, while we can easily use these commands together, *sed by itself* or even using another very useful command called awk, we can leverage Bash itself to shave time and reduce external dependencies in a portable way!

So, how can we do this? Let's begin with a few examples using this Bash syntax:

```bash
#!/bin/bash
# Index zero of VARIABLE is the char 'M' & is 14 bytes long
VARIABLE="My test string"
# ${VARIABLE:startingPosition:optionalLength}
echo ${VARIABLE:3:4}
```

In the preceding example, we can see a special way of calling special substring functionality using `${...}` , where `VARIABLE` is a string variable within your script (or even global), and then the following variable is the `:`. After the `:`, there is the `startingPosition` parameter (remember that strings are just arrays of characters and each character can be addressed by index), and there is another optional semicolon and length parameter (`optionalLength`).

If we ran this script, the output would be:

```
$ bash script.sh
test
```

How is this possible, you may ask? Well, its possible with Bash's equivalent of `substr` (a function in C and many other programming languages), and this is achieved through the usr of the `${...}`syntax. This tells bash to look inside for a variable named `VARIABLE` and then for two parameters: to start at byte/character 3 (technically 4 because arrays start at element 0 in Bash) and a length of 4 (to print only four characters). The result of the echo is `test`.

Can we do more with this, such as removing the last character? Deleting words? Searching? Of course, and all of this is covered in this recipe!

Getting ready

Let's get ready for the exercise by creating some data sets which mimic common daily problems:

```
$ rm -rf testdata; mkdir -p testdata
$ echo "Bob, Jane, Naz, Sue, Max, Tom$" > testdata/garbage.csv
$ echo "Zero, Alpha, Beta, Gama, Delta, Foxtrot#" >> testdata/garbage.csv
$ echo "1000,Bob,Green,Dec,1,1967" > testdata/employees.csv
$ echo "2000,Ron,Brash,Jan,20,1987" >> testdata/employees.csv
$ echo "3000,James,Fairview,Jul,15,1992" >> testdata/employees.csv
```

Using these two CSVs, we are going to:

- Remove the extra spaces on the first two lines of garbage.csv
- Remove the last character from each line in garbage.csv
- Change the case of each character to uppercase in the first two lines of garbage.csv
- Replace Bob with Robert in employees.csv
- Insert a # at the beginning of each line in employees.csv
- Remove the exact date of birth column/field in each line of employees.csv

How to do it...

Let's begin our activity:

1. Open a new terminal and a new file with your preferred editor. Add in the following contents into the new script and save it as builtin-str.sh:

```bash
#!/bin/bash

# Let's play with variable arrays first using Bash's equivalent of
substr

STR="1234567890asdfghjkl"

echo "first character ${STR:0:1}"
echo "first three characters ${STR:0:3}"

echo "third character onwards ${STR: 3}"
echo "forth to sixth character ${STR: 3: 3}"

echo "last character ${STR: -1}"

# Next, can we compare the alphabeticalness of strings?

STR2="abc"
STR3="bcd"
STR4="Bcd"

if [[ $STR2 < $STR3 ]]; then
 echo "STR2 is less than STR3"
else
 echo "STR3 is greater than STR2"
fi
```

```
# Does case have an effect? Yes, b is less than B
if [[ $STR3 < $STR4 ]]; then
 echo "STR3 is less than STR4"
else
 echo "STR4 is greater than STR3"
fi
```

2. Execute the script with `bash builtin-str.sh` and notice how we were able to strip the last character from a string and even compare strings.

3. Again, open a new file called `builtin-strng.sh` and add the following contents into it:

```
#!/bin/bash
GB_CSV="testdata/garbage.csv"
EM_CSV="testdata/employees.csv"
# Let's strip the garbage out of the last lines in the CSV called
garbage.csv
# Notice the forloop; there is a caveat

set IFS=,
set oldIFS = $IFS
readarray -t ARR < ${GB_CSV}

# How many rows do we have?
ARRY_ELEM=${#ARR[@]}
echo "We have ${ARRY_ELEM} rows in ${GB_CSV}"
```

Let's strip the garbage—remove spaces:

```
INC=0
for i in "${ARR[@]}"for i in "${ARR[@]}"
do
:
res="${i//[^ ]}"
TMP_CNT="${#res}"
while [ ${TMP_CNT} -gt 0 ]; do
i=${i/, /,}
TMP_CNT=$[$TMP_CNT-1]
done
ARR[$INC]=$i
INC=$[$INC+1]
done
```

Let's remove the last character from each line:

```
INC=0
for i in "${ARR[@]}"
do
```

```
:
ARR[$INC]=${i::-1}
INC=$[$INC+1]
done
```

Now, let's turn all of the characters into uppercase!

```
INC=0for i in "${ARR[@]}"
do
:
ARR[$INC]=${i^^}
printf "%s" "${ARR[$INC]}"
INC=$[$INC+1]
echo
done

# In employees.csv update the first field to be prepended with a #
character
set IFS=,
set oldIFS = $IFS
readarray -t ARR < ${EM_CSV}

# How many rows do we have?
ARRY_ELEM=${#ARR[@]}

echo;echo "We have ${ARRY_ELEM} rows in ${EM_CSV}"
# Let's add a # at the start of each line
INC=0
for i in "${ARR[@]}"
do
:
ARR[$INC]="#${i}"
printf "%s" "${ARR[$INC]}"
INC=$[$INC+1]
echo
done

# Bob had a name change, he wants to go by the name Robert -
replace it!
echo
echo "Let's make Bob, Robert!"
INC=0
for i in "${ARR[@]}"
do
:
# We need to iterate through Bobs first
ARR[$INC]=${i/Bob/Robert}
printf "%s" "${ARR[$INC]}"
```

```
INC=$[$INC+1]
echo
done
```

We will delete the day in the `birth` column. The field to remove is 5 (but this is really -4):

```
echo;
echo "Lets remove the column: birthday (1-31)"
INC=0
COLUM_TO_REM=4
for i in "${ARR[@]}"
do
  :
# Prepare to also parse the ARR element into another ARR for
# string manipulation
 TMP_CNT=0
 STR=""
 IFS=',' read -ra ELEM_ARR <<< "$i"
 for field in "${ELEM_ARR[@]}"
 do
   # Notice the multiple argument in an if statement
   # AND that we catch the start of it once
   if [ $TMP_CNT -ne 0 ] && [ $TMP_CNT -ne $COLUM_TO_REM ]; then
   STR="${STR},${field}"
   elif [ $TMP_CNT -eq 0 ]
   then
   STR="${STR}${field}"
   fi
   TMP_CNT=$[$TMP_CNT+1]
 done
 ARR[$INC]=$STR
 echo "${ARR[$INC]}"
 INC=$[$INC+1]
done
```

4. Execute the script with `bash builtin-strng.sh` and review the output.

Did you notice all of the opportunities to re-direct input or output? Imagine the possibilities! Furthermore, much of the previous script can be performed using another tool called AWK instead.

How it works...

This recipe is a bit iterative, but it should *re-iterate* (pardon the pun) to demonstrate that Bash has a fair number of functionalities built-in to manipulate strings or any structured data. There is a basic assumption though and that is based on many OSes using C programs:

- A string is an array of characters
- Characters such as ' , ' are the same as any other character
- Therefore, we can evaluate or test for the existence of a character to separate fields from lines and even use this to build arrays

Now, reviewing the steps in this recipe:

1. After running the script, we have the following output in the console:

```
$ builtin-str.sh
first character 1
first three characters 123
third character onwards 4567890asdfghjkl
forth to sixth character 456
last character l
STR2 is less than STR3
STR4 is greater than STR3
```

We began with the string STR="1234567890asdfghjkl" and as the script ran in the first step:

- In the first step, we printed out a single character starting at the zero (0) position. Remember that this is an array, and position 0 is the starting element.
- Next, we retrieved the first three characters to arrive at: 123.
- However, what if we wanted all of the characters after position 3? We would used ${STR: 3} instead of ${STR: 0-3}.
- Then, given the preceding point, if we wanted the characters at position 4 (the forth element in the array, but this is addressed at position three (3) because counting begins at zero (0)), we use ${STR: 3: 3}.
- And finally, to get only the last character, we can use ${STR:-1}.

To finish the first script in the recipe, we had three more strings. If we wished to compare them to each other, we can do so using conditional logic. Remember that bcd is less than BCD.

 Comparing strings using simple Bash constructs can be useful when you want to write a script that quickly compares filenames for a specified execution. For example, run the `001-test.sh` script before `002-test.sh`.

2. In the second half of the recipe, we begin with a long-winded script to duplicate in an easily explained manner. We covered some of the tricks you can use with the Bash shell without using AWK and SED:

```
$ ./builtin-strng.sh
We have 2 rows in testdata/garbage.csv
BOB,JANE,NAZ,SUE,MAX,TOM
ZERO,ALPHA,BETA,GAMA,DELTA,FOXTROT

We have 3 rows in testdata/employees.csv
#1000,Bob,Green,Dec,1,1967
#2000,Ron,Brash,Jan,20,1987
#3000,James,Fairview,Jul,15,1992

Let's make Bob, Robert!
#1000,Robert,Green,Dec,1,1967
#2000,Ron,Brash,Jan,20,1987
#3000,James,Fairview,Jul,15,1992

Lets remove the column: birthday (1-31)
#1000,Robert,Green,Dec,1967
#2000,Ron,Brash,Jan,1987
#3000,James,Fairview,Jul,1992
```

Here is the breakdown of the script, but a brief introduction is required for **arrays, readarray, IFS,** and **oldIFS.** The point of the exercise is to not go into a great lesson on arrays (this will happen later), but to know that you can use them automatically to create dynamic lists of things such as files or lines within a file. They are referred to using the `${ARR[@]}` notation, and each element can be referred to by its index value within the square brackets `[...]`.

The `readarray` command parses the input into an array using the `IFS` and `oldIFS` variables. It separates the data based on a common delimiter (IFS), and oldIFS can maintain the old values, should they be altered:

- In the first step, we use read in the `garbage.csv` (`${GB_CSV}`) and then `${#ARR[@]}` to retrieve the number of elements in the array. We don't use this value, but it is interesting to note the structure of your file and whether it is being read in correctly. Then, for each member of the array, we remove the empty spaces by counting the number of spaces and then removing them with an additional while loop, performing `${i/ /,}` until we're done. The corrected values are then re-inserted into the array.

- In the next step, we use `${i::-1}` and a for loop to remove the last character from each line. Then, the result is re-inserted into the array.

- Using a `for` loop and `ARR[$INC]=${i^^}`, all characters in the array are made uppercase, and we print out the array using `printf` (more on this later in another recipe).

- On to `employees.csv`, we read it into the array again using `readarray`. Then, we add a hash sign (#) to the beginning of each line and re-insert it into the `ARR[$INC]="#${i}"` array.

- Then, we search for the substring `Bob` and replace it with `ARR[$INC]=${i/Bob/Robert}` . To use the built-in search and replace functionality, we use the following syntax: `${variable/valueToFind/valueToReplaceWith}`. Notice that this is also the same premise behind the space removal performed in an earlier step.

- The final step is a bit more complicated and a bit *long in the tooth*, meaning it could be shortened and performed using another tool such as AWK, but for the purpose of an easy to read example—it was written a bit like a C program. Here, we want to remove the actual birthday value (0-31), or column 5 (the index is 4 if we consider that arrays begin at 0). To begin, we iterate through the array using a for loop, and then we use read to take the input value as an array, too! Then, for each field in the array `${ELEM_ARR[@]}`, we then check to see if it is not the first value, and also not the column we wish to remove. We build the correct string via concatenation and then re-insert it into the array before printing each value using `echo`.

Arrays are a data construct and the important thing to think about data is that it can be manipulated in a number of ways. Just like how we split a file line by line to create an array of elements, we can also split those elements into arrays of their own!

Using SED and AWK to remove/replace substrings

Again, when we need to remove a pesky character or remove sections of strings upon occurrence, we can always rely on these two powerful commands: sed and awk. And while we saw that Bash does indeed have a similar functionality built-in, the full tools are able to offer the same and more complex functionality. So, when should we use these tools?

- When we care less about the speed that might be gained by using the built-in functionality of Bash
- When more complex features are needed (when programming constructs like multi-dimensional arrays are required or editing streams)
- When we are focused on portability (Bash might be embedded or a limited version and standalone tools may be required)

Complete books have been written on both SED and AWK, and you can always find far more information online at https://www.gnu.org/software/sed/ and https://www.gnu.org/software/gawk/.

Stream editor (SED) is a handy text manipulation tool that is great for one-liners and offers a simple programming language and regex matching. Alternatively, AWK is also powerful and arguably more than SED. It offers a more complete programming language with a variety of data structures and other constructs. However, it is better suited when working with files such as CSVs, which may contain fields or structured data, but SED can be better when working with text substitutions when working with pipes (for example, grep X | sed ... > file.txt).

Getting ready

Let's get ready for this exercise by creating some data sets which mimic common daily problems:

```
$ rmdir testdata; mkdir -p testdata
$ echo "Bob, Jane, Naz, Sue, Max, Tom$" > testdata/garbage.csv
$ echo "Bob, Jane, Naz, Sue, Max, Tom#" >> testdata/garbage.csv
$ echo "1000,Bob,Green,Dec,1,1967" > testdata/employees.csv
$ echo" 2000,Ron,Brash,Jan,20,1987" >> testdata/employees.csv
$ echo "3000,James,Fairview,Jul,15,1992" >> testdata/employees.csv
```

Using these two CSVs, we are going to:

- Remove the extra spaces on the first two lines of garbage.csv
- Remove the last character from each line in garbage.csv
- Change the case of each character to uppercase in the first two lines of garbage.csv
- Replace Bob with Robert in employees.csv
- Insert a # at the beginning of each line in employees.csv
- Remove the exact date of the birth column/field in each line of employees.csv

How to do it...

As with the exercise using Bash only, we are going to perform a similar recipe as follows:

Create a script called some-strs.sh with the following content and open a new terminal:

```
#!/bin/bash
STR="1234567890asdfghjkl"
echo -n "First character "; sed 's/.//2g' <<< $STR # where N = 2 (N
+1)
echo -n "First three characters "; sed 's/.//4g' <<< $STR

echo -n "Third character onwards "; sed -r 's/.{3}//' <<< $STR
echo -n "Forth to sixth character "; sed -r 's/.{3}//;s/.//4g' <<<
$STR

echo -n "Last character by itself "; sed 's/.*\(.$\)/\1/' <<< $STR
echo -n "Remove last character only "; sed 's/.$//' <<< $STR
```

Execute the script and review the results.

Create another script called `more-strsng.sh` and then execute it:

```sh
#!/bin/sh
GB_CSV="testdata/garbage.csv"
EM_CSV="testdata/employees.csv"
# Let's strip the garbage out of the last lines in the CSV called
garbage.csv
# Notice the forloop; there is a caveat

set IFS=,
set oldIFS = $IFS
readarray -t ARR < ${GB_CSV}

# How many rows do we have?
ARRY_ELEM=${#ARR[@]}
echo "We have ${ARRY_ELEM} rows in ${GB_CSV}"

# Let's strip the garbage - remove spaces
INC=0
for i in "${ARR[@]}"
do
    :
  ARR[$INC]=$(echo $i | sed 's/ //g')
  echo "${ARR[$INC]}"
  INC=$[$INC+1]
done

# Remove the last character and make ALL upper case
INC=0
for i in "${ARR[@]}"
do
    :
  ARR[$INC]=$(echo $i | sed 's/.$//' | sed -e 's/.*/\U&/' )
  echo "${ARR[$INC]}"
  INC=$[$INC+1]
done
```

We want to add a # at the beginning of each line and we will also use the `sed` tool on a per file basis. We just want to strip Bob out and change his name to Robert by manipulating the file in-place:

```sh
set IFS=,
set oldIFS = $IFS
readarray -t ARR < ${EM_CSV}

INC=0
for i in "${ARR[@]}"
```

```
do
  :
 ARR[$INC]=$(sed -e 's/^/#/' <<< $i )
 echo "${ARR[$INC]}"
 INC=$[$INC+1]
done

sed -i 's/Bob/Robert/' ${EM_CSV}
sed -i 's/^/#/' ${EM_CSV} # In place, instead of on the data in the array
cat ${EM_CSV}
# Now lets remove the birthdate field from the files
# Starts to get more complex, but is done without a loop or using cut
awk 'BEGIN { FS=","; OFS="," } {$5="";gsub(",+",",",$0)}1' OFS=, ${EM_CSV}
```

Examine the results—was it simpler to get the results to the recipes that leverage only bash built-in constructs? Likely yes in many situations, IF they are available.

How it works...

After running the two scripts in this recipe, we can see a few items emerge (especially if we compare the built-in Bash functionality for searching, replacing, and substrings).

1. After executing some-strs.sh, we can see the following output in the console:

```
$ bash ./some-strs.sh
First character 1
First three characters 123
Third character onwards 4567890asdfghjkl
Forth to sixth character 456
Last character by itself l
Remove last character only 1234567890asdfghjk
```

At this point, we have seen the echo command used several times, but the -n flag means that we should not automatically create a new line (or carriage return). The <<< re-direct for inputting values as a string has also been previously used, so this should not be new information. Given that, in the first instance, we are using sed like this: sed 's/.//2g' <<< $STR . This script uses sed in very simple ways compared to the plethora of ways you can combine pure sed with regexs. First, you have the command (sed), then the parameters ('s/.//2g'), and then the input (<<< $STR). You can also combine parameters like this: 's/.//2g;s/','/'.'/g' . To get the first character, we use sed in substitute mode (s/) and we retrieve two characters using (/2g), where g stands for global pattern.

The reason it is 2g and not 1g is that a null byte is returned automatically and therefore, if you desire *n* characters then you must specify *n+1* characters. To return the first three characters, we merely change the sed parameters to include 4g instead of 2g.

In the next block of the script, we use sed as follows: sed -r 's/.{3}//' and sed -r '$s/.{3}//;s/.//4g'. You can see that in the first execution of sed, -r is used to specify a regex and so we use the regex to return the string at position 4 (again, those pesky arrays and strings) and everything beyond. In the second instance, we combine starting at the third character but limit the output to only 3 characters.

In the third block of script, we want the final character of the string using sed 's/.*\(.$\)/\1/' and then get the entire string *except* the last character using sed 's/.$//'. In the first instance, we use grouping and wildcards to create the regular expression to return only one character (the last character in the string), and in the second instance, we use the .$ pattern to create an expression that returns everything minus the last character.

It is important to note that search and replace can also be used for deletion operations by specifying an empty value to replace. You can also use the -i flag for in-place edits and to also perform deletion using other flags/parameters.

2. Onto the next script, and after execution, the console should look similar to the following:

```
$ bash more-strsng.sh
We have 2 rows in testdata/garbage.csv
Bob,Jane,Naz,Sue,Max,Tom$
Zero,Alpha,Beta,Gama,Delta,Foxtrot#
BOB,JANE,NAZ,SUE,MAX,TOM
ZERO,ALPHA,BETA,GAMA,DELTA,FOXTROT
#1000,Robert,Green,Dec,1,1967
#2000,Ron,Brash,Jan,20,1987
#3000,James,Fairview,Jul,15,1992
#1000,Robert,Green,Dec,1,1967
#2000,Ron,Brash,Jan,20,1987
#3000,James,Fairview,Jul,15,1992
#1000,Robert,Green,Dec,1967
#2000,Ron,Brash,Jan,1987
#3000,James,Fairview,Jul,1992
```

Again, in the first block of code, we read in the CSV into an array and for each element, we perform a substitution to remove the spaces: `sed 's/ //g'`.

In the second block, again, we iterate through the array, but we remove the last character, `sed 's/.$//'`, and then pipe the output to convert everything to uppercase using `sed -e 's/.*/\U&/'`. In the first part of the pipe, we search for the last character using `.$` and remove it (the `//`). Then, we use an expression to select everything and convert it to upper case using `\U&` (notice that it is a special case allowed by GNU sed). Lowercase can be achieved using `\L&` instead.

In the third block, again, we used a for each loop and a subshell, but we didn't echo the input into `sed`. Sed also takes input like this using the `<<<` input direction. Using `sed -e 's/^/#/'`, we start at the beginning of the string (specified by the `^`) and append a `#`.

Next, for the last three examples, we perform work on the actual files themselves and *not* the arrays loaded into memory by using `sed` with the `-i` flag. This is an important distinction as it will have direct consequences on the files used as input; this is probably what you desire in your scripts anyway! To replace `Bob` with `Robert`, it is the same as removing spaces except we specify the replacement. However, we are performing the replacement on the *entire* input CSV file! We can also add the hash sign for each line in the file, too.

In the final example, we briefly use AWK to show the power of this utility. In this example, we specify the delimiters (FS and OFS) and then we specify the fifth column alongside the `gsub sub` command in the AWK language to remove the column or field. Begin specifies the rules AWK shall use when parsing input and if there are multiple rules, the order received is the order executed.

Alternatively, we can print the first column or field using `awk 'BEGIN { FS=","} { print $1}' testdata/employees.csv` and even the first occurrence by specifying `NR==1` like this: `awk ' BEGIN { FS=","} NR==1{ print $1}'`. Specifying the number or returned records is very useful when using the `grep` command and copious amounts of matches are returned.

 Again, there is so much you can do with AWK and SED. Combined with regular expressions (regexes), explanations and examples of all sorts of usage could fill a book dedicated to each command. You can check out the tools available in the documentation on the web so that you are aware of some platform differences.

Formatting your data/output using echo and printf

Sometimes, finding the string or the exact data you are looking for is the easy part of your task, but formatting the output data is tricky. For example, here are some situations that have subtle elements that need to be altered:

- Echoing output without the newline terminator (\n)
- Echoing raw hexadecimal (hex) data
- Printing raw hexadecimal values and printable ASCII characters
- Concatenating strings
- Escaping specific characters
- Aligning text
- Printing horizontal rules

In addition to tricks, we can also print values to the screen that are also floats as well (in addition to the recipe for math). Wait, what is a hexadecimal number? Yes, another type of data or at least a representation exists. To understand what hexadecimals are, we first need to remember that computers use **binary**, which consists of 1s and 0s (ones and zeros). However, binary is not very friendly to us humans (we use the decimal format when looking at numbers typically), so other representations are sometimes needed, one of which is called **hexadecimal.** As you have probably guessed, it is base 16 so it looks like 0x0 to 0xF (0x0,0x1, ... ,0x9,0xA,0xB, ..., 0XF). Here is an example:

```
$ echo -en '\xF0\x9F\x92\x80\n'
💀
$ printf '\xF0\x9F\x92\x80\n'
💀
```

In the preceding example, both `printf` and `echo` can be used to print raw hex and Unicode characters. Using a Unicode reference, I found the UTF-8 encoding for the **skull** character (F0 9F 92 80) and then formatted it using \xFF. Notice where FF is; it is in each **byte**.

 What can you do knowing about "raw hex" values? Well, you can send characters that the shell can interpret differently, or you can print neat things! See `unicode-table.com` for more detail.

Wait, another term called a **byte**? Yes, and here is another one called a **bit**. A **bit** is the form because it refers to either a 0 or 1, but a **byte is 8 bits** (one byte is made up of eight bits! Get it?).

 As a side note, depending on the platform or measurement—be aware that 1 kilobyte or KB can mean 1,024 Bytes (B) or on many marketing datasheets, 1 KB= 1,000 B. Furthermore, when you see Kb—it does NOT mean kilobytes. It means **Kilo bits!**

 Again, being aware of computational basics such as types of data and conversion between basic data forms is a very useful tool to have in your skill set. It might even be in a job interview or two!

However, we are getting a bit ahead of ourselves—what is echo and printf? Both are commands which you may have seen earlier in this cookbook that allow you to output the contents of variables and more to the console or even to a file. **Echo** is far more "straightforward", but **printf** can provide the same and more functionality using C style parameters. In fact, one of the main features of printf over echo is that printf can format characters, pad them, and even align them.

Alright; let's get to work.

Getting ready

For this exercise, no extra tools or scripts are required—just you, your terminal, and Bash.

How to do it...

Let's begin our activity as follows:

1. Open up a new script called echo-mayhem.sh in your favorite editor and a new terminal. Enter the following contents and then execute the script at the prompt:

```
#!/bin/bash

# What about echo?
echo -n "Currently we have seen the command \"echo\" used before"
echo " in the previous script"
echo
echo -n "Can we also have \t tabs? \r\n\r\n?"
echo " NO, not yet!"
```

```
echo
echo -en "Can we also have \t tabs? \r\n\r\n?"
echo " YES, we can now! enable interpretation of backslash escapes"
echo "We can also have:"
echo -en '\xF0\x9F\x92\x80\n' # We can also use \0NNN for octal
instead of \xFF for hexidecimal
echo "Check the man pages for more info ;)"
```

2. After reviewing the results of echo-mayhem.sh, create another script called printf-mayhem and enter the following contents:

```
#!/bin/bash
export LC_NUMERIC="en_US.UTF-8"
printf "This is the same as echo -e with a new line (\\\n)\n"

DECIMAL=10.0
FLOAT=3.333333
FLOAT2=6.6666 # On purpose two missing values

printf "%s %.2f\n\n" "This is two decimal places: " ${DECIMAL}

printf "shall we align: \n\n %.3f %-.6f\n" ${FLOAT} ${FLOAT2}
printf " %10f %-6f\n" ${FLOAT} ${FLOAT2}
printf " %-10f %-6f\n" ${FLOAT} ${FLOAT2}

# Can we also print other things?
printf '%.0s-' {1..20}; printf "\n"

# How about we print the hex value and a char for each value in a
string?
STR="No place like home!"
CNT=$(wc -c <<< $STR})
TMP_CNT=0

printf "Char Hex\n"

while [ ${TMP_CNT} -lt $[${CNT} -1] ]; do
  printf "%-5s 0x%-2X\n" "${STR:$TMP_CNT:1}" "'${STR:$TMP_CNT:1}"
  TMP_CNT=$[$TMP_CNT+1]
done
```

3. Execute the contents of printf-mayhem.sh and review the contents for subtle differences.

How it works...

While this is a pretty important topic revolving around data types (especially when dealing with math or calculations), we broke the solution to this recipe up into two parts:

1. In step 1, echo is pretty straightforward. We have mentioned in the past that there are special characters and escapes. \t stands for tab \r\n a new line in Windows (although in Linux, \n\n would have sufficed) and again, we could print out a fancy UTF character:

```
$ bash echo-mayhem.sh
Currently we have seen the command "echo" used before in the
previous script

Can we also have \t tabs? \r\n\r\n? NO, not yet!

Can we also have          tabs?

? YES, we can now! enable interpretation of backslash escapes
We can also have:
☻
Check the man pages for more info ;)
```

2. However, the results of step 2 are a bit different, as we can see in the following code. Let's explore this a bit more as it looks like it's a bit more than sloppy alignment:

```
$ bash printf-mayhem.sh
This is the same as echo -e with a new line (\n)
This is two decimal places: 10.00

shall we align:

 3.333 6.666600
   3.333333 6.666600
 3.333333 6.666600
-------------------
Char Hex
N 0x4E
o 0x6F
  0x20
p 0x70
l 0x6C
a 0x61
c 0x63
e 0x65
  0x20
```

```
l 0x6C
i 0x69
k 0x6B
e 0x65
  0x20
h 0x68
o 0x6F
m 0x6D
e 0x65
! 0x21
  0x0
```

3. As we can see, in the preceding step after execution, there are a few interesting things. The first thing we notice is that printf is echo on steroids; it provides the same functionality and far more such as alignment, strings being printed with %s, and decimal places (for example, %.2f). As we dig deeper, we can see that we can limit the number of decimal places using a % after the %tag. Notice the single character usually immediately after the % sign—this is how you format the following parameters. Using a value like %10f, we are dedicating 10 spaces to the value, or rather, the width of 10 characters. If we use %-10, then it means we are aligning the value to the left. And besides the near horizontal rule, which uses expansion, we also "stepped" our way through the string "No place like home!". Using a while loop, we print out each ASCII character using (%-c) with its corresponding hexadecimal value (%-2X).

Notice that even spaces have a hexadecimal (hex) value, and that is 0x20. If you ran the script and got "printf-mayhem.sh: line 26: printf: !: invalid number", this is because you missed the single ' in "'${STR:$TMP_CNT:1}". This signifies how to interpret the returned value as either a string/character or numeric value.

Readying your script for different languages with internationalization

Great, so you have this awesome script, but it's written in standard English and you would like to target those nice people who speak other languages. In some countries like Canada, they (we) have two official languages: English and French. Sometimes, the dual-language component is enforced with legislature and localized language laws.

To get around this, let's imagine a scenario where you are an individual who has written a script that prints out specific strings, but in English first. He/she wishes to have all of the strings inside of variables so that they can be swapped in and out dynamically using system language variables. Here are the basics:

- Create a shell script that utilizes **gettext** and sets the appropriate variables
- Build a **po** file that contains the necessary language definitions
- Install your output language localization file for your script
- Run your script with a language that's different than the one you originally use (by setting the LANG variable)

Before getting started, though, there are two terms that need to be discussed: internationalization (i18n) and localization (L10n). Internationalization is a process that enables translation and localisation/adaptation for a specific script or program, and localization refers to the process of having adapted the program/application for a specific culture.

 The translation of scripts from the start can be an effective way to save time and improve the success of multi-lingual efforts. However, be aware that it can be a time-consuming process if the developers are fluent in only one language, or translation skills are not immediately present.

For example, in English, there are several dialects. In the USA, a product of a process or leftover can be called an **artifact**, but in Canadian English, it may be called an **artefact**. It could go unnoticed (or ignored), but the program could automatically adapt with specific localization.

Getting ready

Let's get ready for the exercise by ensuring that we have the following applications and supporting libraries installed:

```
$ sudo apt-get install -y gettext
```

Next, verify your language environment variables (LANG):

```
$ locale
LANG=en_CA:en
LANGUAGE=en_CA:en
LC_CTYPE="en_CA:en"
LC_NUMERIC="en_CA:en"
LC_TIME="en_CA:en"
LC_COLLATE="en_CA:en"
```

```
LC_MONETARY="en_CA:en"
LC_MESSAGES="en_CA:en"
LC_PAPER="en_CA:en"
LC_NAME="en_CA:en"
LC_ADDRESS="en_CA:en"
LC_TELEPHONE="en_CA:en"
LC_MEASUREMENT="en_CA:en"
LC_IDENTIFICATION="en_CA:en"
LC_ALL=
```

We're assuming your environment probably has some form of English set as the default (en_CA:en is Canadian English)—keep note of the values returned for later!

> You may need to recover your language and locale settings later if something goes wrong. There are many posts on the internet, but a few hints are: $ export LC_ALL="en_US.UTF-8"; sudo locale-gen; and sudo dpkg-reconfigure locales.

How to do it...

Let's begin our activity as follows:

1. Open a new terminal and create a new script called hellobonjour.sh with the following contents:

```
#!/bin/bash
. gettext.sh
function i_have() {
  local COUNT=$1
  ###i18n: Please leave $COUNT as is
  echo -e "\n\t" $(eval_ngettext "I have \$COUNT electronic device"
"I have \$COUNT electronic devices" $COUNT)

}

echo $(gettext "Hello")
echo

echo $(gettext "What is your name?")
echo

###i18n: Please leave $USER as is
echo -e "\t" $(eval_gettext "My name is \$USER" )
echo
```

```
echo $(gettext "Do you have electronics?")

i_have 0
i_have 1
i_have 2
```

2. Run `xgettext` to generate the appropriate strings. We will not use the results, but this is how you can generate a minimalist PO file:

```
$ xgettext --add-comments='##i18n' -o hellobonjour_fr.po
hellobonjour.sh --omit-header
```

3. Copy the already compiled list of strings into the language PO file called `hellobonjour_fr.po`:

```
# Hellobonjour.sh
# Copyright (C) 2017 Ron Brash
# This file is distributed under the same license as the PACKAGE
package.
# Ron Brash <ron.brash@gmail.com>, 2017
# Please ignore my terrible google translations;
# As always, some is better than none!
#, fuzzy
msgid ""
msgstr ""
"Project-Id-Version: 1.0\n"
"Report-Msgid-Bugs-To: i18n@example.com\n"
"POT-Creation-Date: 2017-12-08 12:19-0500\n"
"PO-Revision-Date: YEAR-MO-DA HO:MI+ZONE\n"
"Last-Translator: FULL NAME <EMAIL@ADDRESS>\n"
"Language-Team: French Translator <fr@example.org>\n"
"Language: fr\n"
"MIME-Version: 1.0\n"
"Content-Type: text/plain; charset=iso-8859-1\n"
"Content-Transfer-Encoding: 8bit\n"

#. ##i18n: Please leave $COUNT as is
#: hellobonjour.sh:6
#, sh-format
msgid "I have $COUNT electronic device"
msgid_plural "I have $COUNT electronic devices"
msgstr[0] "J'ai $COUNT appareil electronique"
msgstr[1] "J'ai $COUNT appareils electroniques"

#: hellobonjour.sh:10
msgid "Hello"
msgstr "Bonjour"
```

```
#: hellobonjour.sh:13
msgid "What is your name?"
msgstr "Comment t'appelles tu?"

#. ##i18n: Please leave $USER as is
#: hellobonjour.sh:17
#, sh-format
msgid "My name is $USER"
msgstr "Mon nom est $USER"

#: hellobonjour.sh:20
msgid "Do you have electronics?"
msgstr "Avez-vous des appareils electroniques?"
```

4. Next, using `msgfmt`, compile the PO file into a binary language file with the `.mo` extension and place it in our arbitrary language folder:

```
$ rm -rf locale/fr/LC_MESSAGES
$ mkdir -p locale/fr/LC_MESSAGES
$ sudo msgfmt -o locale/fr/LC_MESSAGES/hellobonjour.mo
hellobonjour_fr.po
```

5. Once you have your language file in place, create the following script with the name of `translator.sh`:

```
#!/bin/bash
./hellobonjour.sh

export TEXTDOMAIN="hellobonjour"
export TEXTDOMAINDIR=`pwd`/locale

export LANGUAGE=fr
./hellobonjour.sh
```

6. Upon executing `translator.sh`, review the results for both executions of `translator.sh`:

```
$ bash translator.sh
```

How it works...

It goes without saying that translation can be a tricky beast, especially when managing encoding and when producing results that make sense at the human language level. Furthermore, even a slight change in the value within the script can break the PO file and the resulting script will not be fully translated (sometimes, not even at all).

Take care not to break the *keys* when making modifications to the scripts at a later date.

1. Step one is fairly straightforward—you just create a script. If you run the script, you will see purely an English result, but at least the plural and non-plural output is correct. Notice `.  gettext.sh`; this line preps `gettext` to prepare and to be ran for internationalization/localization. In the script, we also use `gettext`, `eval_gettext`, and `eval_ngettext`. These are functions that allow the translation to occur. Use `gettext` for simple translations, `eval_gettext` for a translation that contains a variable, and `eval_ngettext` when you have translations that contain plural objects. As you may have noticed, `eval_ngettext` is a bit more complex: `$(eval_ngettext "I have \$COUNT electronic device" "I have \$COUNT electronic devices" $COUNT)`. The first parameter for `eval_ngettext` is the singular translation, the second is the plural, and the count is the variable used to determine if a singular or plural value is used. Variables are referred to in the original script with an escape `\$COUNT`, and the translated string that contains the variable will appear as `$COUNT` inside of the translation file without the escape:

   ```
   ./hellobonjour.sh
   Hello

   What is your name?

       My name is rbrash

   Do you have electronics?

       I have 0 electronic devices

       I have 1 electronic device

       I have 2 electronic devices
   ```

2. In step two, we create the language file called a PO file using `xgettext`. PO is short for Portable Object. Notice that we omitted the header because it will produce extra output. It is particularly useful when you want to write notes, versions, and even specify the encoding used.

3. Instead of writing the translations from scratch, we used our trusty friend Google translate to produce a few basic translations and we copy them over the output from xgettext. Xgettext created almost the same file! Notice msgid, msgstr, msgplural, and msgstr[...]. Msgid and msgid_plural are used to match the original values as if they were a key. For example, as the script runs, gettext sees "I have $COUNT electronic device", and then knows to output a specific translation that matches that same msgid:

```
msgid "I have $COUNT electronic device"
msgid_plural "I have $COUNT electronic devices"
msgstr[0] ".."
```

4. hellobonjour_fr.po contains all of our translations, and now we can use a command called msgfmt, which is used to produce a MO file or Machine Object. If you open this file with an editor like vi, you will notice that it contains a bunch of symbols representing binary and the strings. This file should not be edited, but rather the input PO file itself.

5. Next, we create a file called translator.sh. It runs hellobonjour.sh and contains a few lines that set three important variables: TEXTDOMAIN, TEXTDOMAINDIR, and LANGUAGE. TEXTDOMAIN is typically the variable used to describe the binary or shell script (think of it as a namespace), and TEXTDOMAINDIR is the directory for gettext to look for the translation. Notice that it's in a local relative directory, and not /usr/share/locale (which it could be). Finally, we set LANGUAGE to fr for French.

6. When we execute translator.sh, hellobonjour.sh is run twice and outputs once in English, and the second time in French:

```
$ bash translator.sh

Hello

What is your name?

    My name is rbrash

Do you have electronics?

    I have 0 electronic devices

    I have 1 electronic device

    I have 2 electronic devices
Bonjour
```

```
Comment t'appelles tu?

    Mon nom est rbrash

Avez-vous des appareils electroniques?

    J'ai 0 appareils electroniques

    J'ai 1 appareil electronique

    J'ai 2 appareils electroniques
```

Do not use the old format of $"my string" for translation. It is subject to security risks!

Calculating statistics and reducing duplicates based on file contents

At first glance, calculating statistics based on the contents of a file might not be among the most interesting tasks one could accomplish with Bash scripting, however, it can be useful in several circumstances. Let's imagine that our program takes user input from several commands. We could calculate the length of the input to determine if it is too little or too much. Alternatively, we could also determine the size of a string to determine buffer sizes for a program written in another programming language (such as C/C++):

```
$ wc -c <<< "1234567890"
11 # Note there are 10 chars + a new line or carriage return \n
$ echo -n "1234567890" | wc -c
10
```

We can use commands like wc to calculate the number of occurrences of words, total number of lines, and many other actions in conjunction to the functionality provided by your script.

Better yet, what if we used a command called **strings** to output all printable ASCII strings to a file? The strings program will output *every* occurrence of a string—even if there are duplicates. Using other programs like `sort` and `uniq` (or a combination of the two), we can also sort the contents of a file and reduce duplicates if we wanted to calculate the number of *unique* lines within a file:

```
$ strings /bin/ls > unalteredoutput.txt
$ ls -lah unalteredoutput.txt
-rw-rw-r-- 1 rbrash rbrash 22K Nov 24 11:17 unalteredoutput.txt
$ strings /bin/ls | sort -u > sortedoutput.txt
$ ls -lah sortedoutput.txt
-rw-rw-r-- 1 rbrash rbrash 19K Nov 24 11:17 usortedoutput.txt
```

Now that we know a few basic premises of why we may need to perform some basic statistics, let's carry on with the recipe.

Getting ready

Let's get ready for the exercise by creating a single dataset:

```
$ mkdir -p testdata
$ cat /etc/hosts > testdata/duplicates.txt; cat /etc/hosts >>
testdata/duplicates.txt
```

How to do it...

We have already seen most of these concepts already and even `wc` itself in one of the previous recipes, so let's get started:

1. Open a terminal and run the following commands:

```
$ wc -l testdata/duplicates.txt
$ wc -c testdata/duplicates.txt
```

2. As you may have noticed, the output has the filename included. Can we remove it with AWK? Absolutely, but we can also remove it with a command called `cut`. The `-d` flag stand, for delimiter and we would like to have a field (specified by `-f1`):

```
$ wc -c testdata/duplicates.txt | cut -d ' ' -f1
$ wc -c testdata/duplicates.txt | awk '{ print $1 }'
```

3. Imagine that we have a massive file full of strings. Could we reduce the returned results? Of course, but let's use the `sort` command first to sort the elements contained in `testdata/duplicates.txt` and then use `sort` to produce a list of only the unique elements:

```
$ sort testdata/duplicates.txt
$ sort -u testdata/duplicates.txt
$ sort -u testdata/duplicates.txt | wc -l
```

How it works...

Overall, no truly abstract concepts were introduced in this script, except for counting numbers of occurrences and the benefit of sort. Sorting can be a time-consuming process to reduce unneeded or extra data or when the order matters, but it can also be rewarding when performing bulk operations, and pre-processing yields faster returns overall.

Onward and upward to the recipe:

1. Running these two `wc` commands will produce both a character and line count of the file `testdata/duplicates.txt`. It also begins to show another problem. The data can be padded with the filename prefixed with a space:

```
$ wc -l testdata/duplicates.txt
18 testdata/duplicates.txt
$ wc -c testdata/duplicates.txt
438 testdata/duplicates.txt
```

2. In step 2, we use `awk` and `cut` to remove the second field. The `cut` command is a useful command for trimming strings, which may be delimited or merely using hard-coded values such as remove X characters. Using `cut`, `-d` stands for delimiter, the space in this example (' '), and `-f1` stands for field 1:

```
$ wc -c testdata/duplicates.txt | cut -d ' ' -f1
438
$ wc -c testdata/duplicates.txt | awk '{ print $1 }'
438
```

3. In the final step, we run the `sort` command three times. We run it once to merely sort the elements in `testdata/duplicates.txt`, but then we use the `-u` to sort and keep only unique elements, and the `final` command counts the number of unique elements. Of course, the returned value is 9 because we had 18 lines in the original duplicates file:

```
$sort testdata/duplicates.txt

127.0.0.1 localhost
127.0.0.1 localhost
127.0.1.1 moon
127.0.1.1 moon
::1 ip6-localhost ip6-loopback
::1 ip6-localhost ip6-loopback
fe00::0 ip6-localnet
fe00::0 ip6-localnet
ff00::0 ip6-mcastprefix
ff00::0 ip6-mcastprefix
ff02::1 ip6-allnodes
ff02::1 ip6-allnodes
ff02::2 ip6-allrouters
ff02::2 ip6-allrouters
# The following lines are desirable for IPv6 capable hosts
# The following lines are desirable for IPv6 capable hosts

$ sort -u testdata/duplicates.txt

127.0.0.1 localhost
127.0.1.1 moon
::1 ip6-localhost ip6-loopback
fe00::0 ip6-localnet
ff00::0 ip6-mcastprefix
ff02::1 ip6-allnodes
ff02::2 ip6-allrouters
# The following lines are desirable for IPv6 capable hosts
$ sort -u testdata/duplicates.txt | wc -l
9
```

Using file attributes with conditional logic

Earlier in this book, we touched upon various tests for strings, numbers, and variables. Using a similar concept built into Bash, we can also use various attributes to test against files and directories. This extends upon the introduction conditional logic to perform tests on files. Does an example exist? Is it a directory? and so on.

For a moment, though, couldn't we just use the results from executing and checking the return code? Absolutely! This is another method you can use, especially if you are using a version of Bash that supports all of Bashes features. It is just another way to "skin the rabbit".

Let's start off first with some of the common flags, which return true if:

- `-e`: The file exists
- `-f`: This is a regular file and not a directory or device file
- `-s`: The file is not empty or zero in size
- `-d`: This is a directory
- `-r`: This has read permissions
- `-w`: This has write permissions
- `-x`:This has execute permissions
- `-O`: This is the owner of the file the current user
- `-G`: This executes the user if they have the same group as yours
- `f1 (- nt, -ot, -ef) f2`: Refers to if `f1` is newer than `f2`, older than `f2`, or are hard-linked to the same file

 There is more information available on file test operations in the GNU Bash manual: `https://www.gnu.org/software/bash/manual/html_node/Bash-Conditional-Expressions.html`.

Getting ready

Let's get ready for the exercise by creating a few text files and directories, and adding some content:

```
$ cd ~/
$ mkdir -p fileops
$ touch fileops/empty.txt
$ echo "abcd1234!!" > fileops/string.txt
$ echo "yieldswordinthestone" > fileops/swordinthestone.txt
$ touch fileops/read.txt fileops/write.txt fileops/exec.txt fileops/all.txt
$ chmod 111 fileops/exec.txt; chmod 222 fileops/write.txt; chmod 444
fileops/read.txt; fileops/all.txt;chmod 777 fileops/all.txt
$ sudo useradd bob
$ echo "s the name" > fileops/bobs.txt
$ sudo chown bob.bob fileops/bobs.txt
```

This recipe is about performing some simple file tests and to combine some of the other knowledge from earlier recipes on conditional logic, but with a twist—using user input from the CLI and file permissions.

> Notice the commands chmod, useradd, and chmod. Chmod is the command you may use to change the permissions of files for execution and more.

How to do it...

Let's begin our activity as follows:

1. Open a new terminal and start an editor of your choice and create a new script. The following is a code snippet from the script:

```
#!/bin/bash
FILE_TO_TEST=""

function permissions() {
  echo -e "\nWhat are our permissions on this $2?\n"
  if [ -r $1 ]; then
    echo -e "[R] Read"
  fi
  if [ -w $1 ]; then
    echo -e     "[W] Write"
  fi
  if [ -x $1 ]; then
    echo -e "[X] Exec"
  fi
}

function file_attributes() {

  if [ ! -s $1 ]; then
    echo "\"$1\" is empty"
  else
    FSIZE=$(stat --printf="%s" $1 2> /dev/null)
    RES=$?
    if [ $RES -eq 1 ]; then
      return
    else
      echo "\"$1\" file size is: ${FSIZE}\""
    fi
  fi
```

```
    if [ ! -O $1 ]; then
      echo -e "${USER} is not the owner of \"$1\"\n"
    fi
    if [ ! -G $1 ]; then
      echo -e "${USER} is not among the owning group(s) for \"$1\"\n"
    fi
    permissions $1 "file"
}
```

2. Execute the script and try to access the various files, including the directories and files that do not exist. What do you notice?

3. Remove the folder now with this command:

```
$ sudo rm -rf fileops
```

How it works...

First, before digging into the script itself or even the attributes/properties of files, we need to know a few things about Linux and its sibling operating systems:

- Files and directories can be owned. This means that they can have an owner (user) and groups associated with their ownership. For this, we can use the chown and chgrp commands.
- Files and directories can have different permissions applied to them. This means that they may be executable, readable, writable, and/or everything. For this, we can use the chmod command and the appropriate permission setting.
- Files and directories can also be empty.

Great! Furthermore, there are two more concepts that need to be introduced:

- The read command, which is used to wait for user input and read it into a variable. It is also useful for "pause" functionality in scripts.
- Recursive functions. Notice that inside of the script unless it exits or the user presses *ctl* + *C*, the script keeps calling a particular function. This is recursion and it will continue unless stopped or a limit is applied.

At this point, we also know functions, parameters, input/output, return codes, subshells, and conditional logic. You may not have noticed the ! character, and this is used to negate a statement. For example, if we test for the existence of fileops/bobs.txt using the -e test operator, it will return true. Instead, we can test for the opposite, which is that fileops/bobs.txt is non-existent.

The same logic as inverting or negating statements can also be achieved using if/else functionality, but it can sometimes improve script "readability" and "flow". Ultimately, the choice to use inversion is up to the script writer.

1. Great! We have created our script and are ready to execute it.
2. Upon executing the script, we are greeted with:

```
$ ./files-extended.sh
Welcome to the file attributes tester

To exit, press CTRL + C

What is the complete path of the file you want to inspect?
 #
```

If we look back at the setup for this recipe, we know that we created several files inside of the directory `fileops/` and that a few of them have different permissions, one of which is owned by a user named `Bob`.

Let's try a few executions (in order) :

- `fileops/bobs.txt`
- `fileops/write.txt`
- `fileops/exec.txt`
- `fileops/all.txt`
- `thisDoesNotExist.txt`:

```
# fileops/bobs.txt

"fileops/bobs.txt" file size is: 11"
rbrash is not the owner of "fileops/bobs.txt"

rbrash is not among the owning group(s) for "fileops/bobs.txt"

What are our permissions on this file?

[R] Read

What is the complete path of the file you want to inspect?
 # fileops/write.txt

"fileops/write.txt" is empty

What are our permissions on this file?
```

```
[W] Write

What is the complete path of the file you want to inspect?
 # fileops/exec.txt

"fileops/exec.txt" is empty

What are our permissions on this file?

{X] Exec

What is the complete path of the file you want to inspect?
 # fileops/all.txt

"fileops/all.txt" is empty

What are our permissions on this file?

[R] Read
[W] Write
{X] Exec

What is the complete path of the file you want to inspect?
 # fileops

Directory "fileops" has children:

all.txt
bobs.txt
empty.txt
exec.txt
read.txt
string.txt
swordinthestone.txt
write.txt

What are our permissions on this directory?

[R] Read
[W] Write
{X] Exec

What is the complete path of the file you want to inspect?
 # thisDoesNotExist.txt

Error: "thisDoesNotExist.txt" does not exist!
$
```

As `thisDoesNotExist.txt` does not exist, the script abruptly exits and places you back at the console prompt. We tested with the various flags, negation, ownership, and even our ever useful utility `xargs`.

Reading delimited data and altered output format

Every day, we open many files in many different formats. However, when thinking about large amounts of data, it is always a good practice to use standard formats. One of these is called **Comma Separated Values**, or CSVs, and it uses a comma (,) to separate **elements** or **delimit** on each row. This is particularly useful when you have large amounts of data or **records**, and that data will be used in a scripted fashion. For example, in every school semester, Bob, the system administrator, needs to create a series of new users and set their information. Bob also gets a standardized CSV (like in the following snippet) from the people in charge of attendance:

```
Rbrash,Ron,Brash,01/31/88,+11234567890,rbrash@acme.com,FakePassword9000
...
```

If Bob the administrator wishes to only read this information into an array and create users, it is relatively trivial for him to parse a CSV and create each record in one single scripted action. This allows Bob to focus his time and effort on other important issues such as troubleshooting end-user WiFi issues.

While this is a trivial example, these same files may be in different forms with **delimiters** (the , or $ sign, for example), different data, and different structures. However, each file works on the premise that each line is a record that needs to be read into some structure (whatever it may be) in SQL, Bash arrays, and so on:

```
Line1Itself: Header (optional and might not be present)
Line2ItselfIsOneREc:RecordDataWithDelimiters:endline (windows \r\n, in
Linux \n)
....
```

In the preceding example of a pseudo CSV, there is a header, which may be optional (not present), and then several lines (each being a record). Now, for Bob to parse the CSV, he has many ways to do this, but he may use specialized functions that apply a strategy such as:

```
$ Loop through each item until done
for each line in CSV:
    # Do something with the data such as create a user
    # Loop through Next item if it exists
```

To read in the data, Bob or yourself may resort to using:

- For loops and arrays
- A form of iterator
- Manually walking through each line (not efficient)

Once any input data has been read in, the next step is to do something with the data itself. Is it to be transformed? Is it to be used immediately? Sanitized? Stored? Or converted to another format? Just like Bob, there are many things that can be performed using the data read in by the script.

In regards to outputting the data, we can also convert it to XML, JSON, or even insert it into a database as SQL. Unfortunately, this process requires being able to know at least two things: the format of the input data and the format of the output data.

Knowing common data formats and how they often have validation applied can be a great asset when building automated scripts and identifying any changes in the future. Enforcement of data validation also has several benefits and can help save the day when all of a sudden the script breaks without warning!

This recipe aims at walking you through reading a trivial CSV and outputting the data into some arbitrary formats.

Getting ready

Let's get ready for the exercise by creating some data sets which mimic common daily problems:

```
$ cd ~/
$ echo
$ echo -e "XML_HDR='<?xml version="1.0"
encoding="UTF-8"?>'\\nSRT_CONTR='<words
type="greeting">'\\nEND_CONTR='</words>'" > xml-parent.tpl
$ echo -e "ELM='\"<word lang=\"\$1\">\"\$2\"</word>\"'" > word.tpl
$ echo -e "\"EN\",\"Hello\"\n\"FR\",\"Bonjour\"" > words.csv
```

In Bash, the single quote (') is used for literal strings. In this case, we want every part of the string to be present without escaping slashes and double quotes.

To operate this script, you have the following applications installed for use within the script:

```
$ sudo apt-get install npm sed awk
$ sudo npm install -g xml2json-command
$ sudo ln -s /usr/bin/nodejs /usr/bin/node
```

How to do it...

Let's begin our activity as follows:

1. Open a terminal and create the `data-csv-to-xml.sh` script with the following contents. Then, execute the script after saving it using `$ bash data-csv-to-xml.sh`:

```bash
#!/bin/bash

# Import template variables
source xml-parent.tpl
source word.tpl

OUTPUT_FILE="words.xml"
INPUT_FILE="words.csv"
DELIMITER=','

# Setup header
echo ${XML_HDR} > ${OUTPUT_FILE}
echo ${SRT_CONTR} >> ${OUTPUT_FILE}

# Enter content
echo ${ELM} | \
sed '{:q;N;s/\n/\\n/g;t q}'| \
awk \
'{ print "awk \x27 BEGIN{FS=\"'${DELIMITER}'\"}{print "$0"}\x27
'${INPUT_FILE}'"}' | \
 sh >> ${OUTPUT_FILE}

# Append trailer
echo ${END_CONTR} >> ${OUTPUT_FILE}

cat ${OUTPUT_FILE}
```

2. Examine the output, but be aware that "pretty" XML isn't necessary and in fact, we don't even need to have the XML on multiple lines. If pure data is required for a web application, the extra new lines and tabs are unnecessary data to be transmitted.

3. Create another script named `data-xml-to-json.sh` with the following contents. Then, execute the script after saving it using `$ data-xml-to-json.sh`:

```
!#/bin/bash
INPUT_FILE"words.xml"
OUTPUT_FILE="words.json"

# Easy one line!
xml2json < ${INPUT_FILE} ${OUTPUT_FILE}
```

4. Review the output and see how it easy it is! Are there areas you could improve on in both of the scripts?

How it works...

We have already discussed several important aspects such as the power of the SED and AWK commands, and even CSVs, but we have not discussed the importance of being able to **transform** the format and structure of data. CSVs are a fundamental and very common format of data, but unfortunately, it isn't the best choice for some applications, so we may use XML or JSON. Here are two scripts (or rather one script and one tool) that can convert our original data into various formats:

1. When executing `data-csv-to-xml.sh`, we notice several things: we utilize two source template files, which can be altered for flexibility, and then a large piped command that leverages sed and AWK. On input, we take each of the CSV values and build a `<word lang="x">Y</word>` XML element using the format template inside of `word.tpl`, where `$0` is field one and `$1` is field two. The script will produce a `words.csv` and output the following:

```
$ bash data-csv-to-xml.sh
<?xml version="1.0" encoding="UTF-8"?>
<words type="greeting">
<word lang="EN">"Hello"</word>
<word lang="FR">"Bonjour"</word>
</words>
```

2. In the second script, we merely take `words.xml` as input into the command `xml2json`. The output will be in JSON format. Cool hey?

```
!#/bin/bash
{
  "words": {
    "type": "greeting",
    "word": [
      {
        "lang": "EN",
        "$t": "\"Hello\""
      },
      {
        "lang": "FR",
        "$t": "\"Bonjour\""
      }
    ]
  }
}
```

The differences and reasons between all three formats of data (CSV, XML, and JSON) is left as an exercise for the reader to discover. Another exercise to explore is performing data validation to ensure integrity and constraints on data. For example, XML can use XSD schemas to enforce data limits.

Understanding and Gaining File System Mastery

3

In this chapter, we will introduce the following:

- Viewing files from various angles – head, tail, less, and more
- Searching for files by name and/or extension
- Creating a diff of two files and patching
- Creating symbolic links and using them effectively
- Crawling filesystem directories and printing a tree
- Finding and deleting duplicate files or directories
- Joining and splitting files at arbitrary positions
- Generating datasets and random files of various size

Introduction

In this chapter, we will extend some of the contents from Chapter 2, *Acting Like a Typewriter and File Explorer*, but aim to make you even stronger when creating, viewing, and managing files. After all, how does one look at a very large file? Find external software dependencies of a binary and manipulate files? Surely, these tasks are cornerstones in a number of tasks any one developer, administrator, or power user can think of.

For example, Bob the reader has already been introduced to VI, and perhaps he has his own GUI editor or application, such as Open Office, but what happens if that editor likes to crash upon opening a full file? Can he just look at the starting few lines? Absolutely. Can he split that file (if the structure is known like a CSV) at X number of lines? Again, absolutely!

All of these things are not impossible, and the list of activities Bob can do can continue on forever. The idea of this chapter is to give you a segue into some of the things you can do if life isn't going your way or you need quick access/control over the files on your system.

> The scripts for this chapter can be found at `https://github.com/` `PacktPublishing/Bash-Cookbook/tree/master/chapter%2003`.

Viewing files from various angles – head, tail, less, and more

As of this very moment, your system likely has many text files of various sizes including a never ending log file being written too. You might even have several large files containing copious amounts of code (such as the Linux kernel or a software project) and would like to quickly view them from the console without slowing your system down to a halt.

To do this, there are four essential commands that should be able to provide you more than enough functionality for their purposes:

- **Head**: Can be used to output the beginning lines of a file
- **Tail**: Can be used to output the end or tail of a file (continuously as well)
- **More**: A tool used as a *pager* to view large files page by page/line by line
- **Less**: Is the same as more, but it has more features, including backwards scrolling

> Sometimes, you may see the command `more` on embedded systems and not the `less` command. This is because the less command is larger than `more`. Does your head hurt yet?

Getting ready

Besides having a terminal open, several large text files are needed for this recipe. If you have some already, great; if not, install the following:

```
$ wget http://www.randomtext.me/download/txt/lorem/ol-20/98-98.txt
$ fmt 98-98.txt > loremipsum.txt
```

The `fmt` command is a simple optimal text formatter. It is used to clean up the output a bit for better results on the command line.

How to do it...

Open a terminal and run the following commands:

```
$ cat loremipsum.txt
$ head loremipsum.txt
$ head -n 1 loremipsum.txt
$ tail loremipsum.txt
$ tail -n 1 loremipsum.txt
```

Interestingly enough, the `tail` command has a feature that is different than the `head` command: it can monitor the tail end of a file forever until the command is exited or killed when using the `-f` or `-F` flags. Run the following command:

```
$ tail -F /var/log/kern.log
```

Keeping the `tail` command running, try disconnecting your wireless or Ethernet port. What do you see?

Press *Ctrl* + *C* to quit `tail` and run the following command:

```
$ more loremipsum.txt
```

Pressing the spacebar or *Enter* on your keyboard will progress through the file until the end. Pressing `q` will immediately exit `more` and return you to the console prompt.

Next, try the following command:

```
$ less loremipsum.txt
```

Try navigating through the file using *pg up*, *pg dn*, the up and down arrow keys, and *Enter* and the spacebar. Notice anything?

How it works...

Before proceeding, note that the contents of the `loremipsum.txt` file will be different for every instance downloaded. **Lorem Ipsum** is pseudo random text that is used in a variety of text-related duties, often as placeholder values because it *looks* to be a language of sorts and is useful where the human brain is disturbed by copy and paste stub text.

Great! Let's get started:

1. In the first step, the commands should produce similar results to the following block (for brevity, we excluded much of the output to keep the recipe coherent), but notice that head begins at the beginning, or *head*, of `loremipsum.txt`, and tail begins at the end, or *tail*, of `loremipsum.txt`. When we specify the -n flag with a decimal number such as 1, both utilities will output a single line or whatever number of lines is entered:

```
$ cat loremipsum.txt

Feugiat orci massa inceptos proin adipiscing urna vestibulum
hendrerit morbi convallis commodo porta magna, auctor cras nulla
ligula
sit vehicula primis ultrices duis rutrum cras feugiat sit facilisis
fusce placerat sociosqu amet cursus quisque praesent mauris
facilisis,
egestas curabitur imperdiet sit elementum ornare sed class ante
pharetra
in, nisi luctus sit accumsan iaculis eu platea sit ullamcorper
platea
erat convallis orci volutpat curabitur nostra tellus erat non nisl
condimentum, cubilia lacinia eget rhoncus pharetra euismod sagittis
morbi risus, nisl scelerisque fringilla arcu auctor turpis
ultricies
imperdiet nibh eget felis leo enim auctor sed netus ultricies sit
fames
...
$ head loremipsum.txt
 Feugiat orci massa inceptos proin adipiscing urna vestibulum
hendrerit morbi convallis commodo porta magna, auctor cras nulla
ligula
sit vehicula primis ultrices duis rutrum cras feugiat sit facilisis
fusce placerat sociosqu amet cursus quisque praesent mauris
facilisis,
egestas curabitur imperdiet sit elementum ornare sed class ante
pharetra in
$ head -n 1 loremipsum.txt
 Feugiat orci massa inceptos proin adipiscing urna vestibulum
```

```
$ tail loremipsum.txt
euismod torquent primis mattis velit aptent risus accumsan cubilia
eros
justo ad sodales dapibus tempor, donec mauris erat at lacinia
senectus
luctus venenatis mollis ullamcorper ante mollis nisl leo
sollicitudin
felis congue tempus nam curabitur viverra venenatis quis, felis
pretium
enim posuere elit bibendum dictumst, bibendum mattis blandit
sociosqu
adipiscing cursus quisque augue facilisis vehicula metus taciti
conubia
odio proin rutrum aliquam lorem, erat lobortis etiam eget risus
lectus
sodales mauris blandit, curabitur velit risus litora tincidunt
inceptos
nam ipsum platea felis mi arcu consequat velit viverra, facilisis
 ulputate semper vitae suspendisse aliquam, amet proin potenti
semper
$ tail -n 1 loremipsum.txt
 ulputate semper vitae suspendisse aliquam, amet proin potenti
semper
```

2. In the second step, we discover a key difference between the head and tail commands. Tail is able to monitor a file while continuously dumping the tail contents of the file to standard out (stdout). If the file has a read error, or is moved/rotated out, -f (lowercase) will often stop outputting information, while -F will reopen the file and continue outputting the contents.

   -F instead of -f is usually the desired option between the two if tailing system logs.

3. With tail still running in continuous mode, several new entries should appear among the output. This sample is from when a system's wireless adapter was forced to reconnect to a standard access point (AP):

```
Dec 8 14:21:40 moon kernel: userif-2: sent link up event.
Dec 8 14:21:40 moon kernel: wlp3s0: authenticate with
18:d6:c7:fa:26:b0
Dec 8 14:21:40 moon kernel: wlp3s0: send auth to 18:d6:c7:fa:26:b0
(try 1/3)
Dec 8 14:21:40 moon kernel: wlp3s0: authenticated
Dec 8 14:21:40 moon kernel: wlp3s0: associate with
```

```
18:d6:c7:fa:26:b0 (try 1/3)
Dec 8 14:21:40 moon kernel: wlp3s0: RX AssocResp from
18:d6:c7:fa:26:b0 (capab=0x411 status=0 aid=1)
Dec 8 14:21:40 moon kernel: wlp3s0: associated
Dec 8 14:21:40 moon kernel: bridge-wlp3s0: device is wireless,
enabling SMAC
Dec 8 14:21:40 moon kernel: userif-2: sent link down event.
Dec 8 14:21:40 moon kernel: userif-2: sent link up event.
```

4. After killing the `tail` command, your console should be back at the prompt again: $.

5. Running `more` and using the spacebar or *Enter* keys will progress output through the entire `loremipsum.txt` file. The `more` command is only able to view from beginning to end, and not back and forth.

6. The `less` command is certainly more powerful and offers the user to be able to navigate through `loremipsum.txt` using several key combinations. It also offers search facilities among other features.

Searching for files by name and/or extension

When we have large number of files available for viewing, sometimes we need to find a file among many without using the GUI searching tools or provide a better set of granular filters to reduce returned results. To search on the command line, there are a few facilities/commands we can use:

- `locate` (also a sibling of the `updatedb` command): Used to find files more efficiently using an index of files
- `find`: Used to find files with specific attributes, extensions, and even names within a specific directory

The `find` command is far more suitable for the command line and widespread (often being on embedded devices), but the `locate` command is a common facility for use on desktops, laptops, and servers. Locate is far more simpler and involves recursively indexing all of the files it is configured to keep track of and it can generate very quick file listings. The file index can be updated using the following command:

```
$ sudo updatedb
```

Updating the database for the first time or after large amounts of files have been created, moved, or copied may result in longer than average times to update the database. One particular mechanism to keep the database frequently up to date automatically is through the use of **cron scheduler**. More about this topic will be covered later.

The `locate` command can also be used to test for the existence of a file before reporting its location (the database may be out of date), and also limit the number of entries returned.

As noted, `find` does not have a fancy database, but it does have a number of user configurable flags, which can be passed to it at the time of execution. Some of the most commonly used flags used with the `find` command are as follows:

- `-type`: This is used to specify the type of file, which can be either file or directory
- `-delete`: This is used to delete files, but may not be present, which means that `exec` will be required
- `-name`: This is used to specify searching by name functionality
- `-exec`: This is used to specify what else to do upon match
- `-{a,c,m}time`: This is used to search for things such as time of access, creation, and modification
- `-d, -depth`: This is used to specify the depth searching may delve recursively into
- `-maxdepth`: This is used to specify the maximum depth per recursion
- `-mindepth`: This is used to specify the minimum depth when recursively searching
- `-L, -H, -P`: In order, `-L` follow symbolic links, `-H` does not follow symbolic links except in specific cases, and `-P` never follows symbolic links
- `-print, -print0`: These commands are used to print the name of the current file on a standard output
- `!, -not`: This is used to specify logical operations such as match everything, but not on this criteria
- `-i`: This is used to specify user interaction on a match such as `-iname test`

Please be aware that your platform may not support all of GNU find's features. This may be the case with limited shells for embedding, resource constraints, or security reasons.

Getting ready

Besides having a terminal open, several large text files are needed for this recipe. If you have some already, great; if not, install the following:

```
$ sudo apt-get install locate manpages manpages-posix
$ sudo updatedb
$ git clone
https://github.com/PacktPublishing/Linux-Device-Drivers-Development.git
Linux-Device-Drivers-Development # Another Packt title
$ mkdir -p ~/emptydir/makesure
```

If a file is not found using the `locate` command, the database might be simply out of date and needs to be re-ran. It is possible that `updatedb` is also not indexing partitions such as those contained on removable media (USB sticks), and the file may be present there instead of the regular system partitions.

In preparation for this recipe, be aware that two concepts were inadvertently introduced: `git` and `manpages`. Manpages are among one of the oldest forms of help documentation available in Linux, and git is a version control system that simplifies management, versioning, and distribution of files such as code. Knowing how to use either is certainly beneficial, but beyond the scope of this book. For more information about git, check out another Packt book: *GIT Version Control Cookbook*.

How to do it...

1. Open a terminal and run the following commands in order to understand the `locate` command:

```
$ locate stdio.h
$ sudo touch /usr/filethatlocatedoesntknow.txt
/usr/filethatlocatedoesntknow2.txt
$ sudo sh -c 'echo "My dear Watson ol\'boy" >
/usr/filethatlocatedoesntknow.txt'
$ locate filethatlocatedoes
$ sudo updatedb
$ locate filethatlocatedoesntknow
```

2. Next, run the following commands to demonstrate some of the power of `find`:

```
$ sudo find ${HOME} -name ".*" -ls
$ sudo find / -type d -name ".git"
$ find ${HOME} -type f \( -name "*.sh" -o -name "*.txt" \)
```

3. Next, we can chain the `find` commands together with `&&` and ultimately perform an `exec` instead of piping the output to another process, command, or script. Try the following:

```
$ find . -type d -name ".git" && find . -name ".gitignore" && find
. -name ".gitmodules"
$ sudo find / -type f -exec grep -Hi 'My dear Watson ol boy' {} +
```

4. Finally, one of the most common uses of find is to delete files using either the built-in `-delete` flag or by using `exec` combined with rm `-rf`:

```
$ find ~/emptydir -type d -empty -delete
$ find Linux-Device-Drivers-Development -name ".git*" -exec rm -rf
{} \;
```

How it works...

Repeat after me—"*locate is simple* and needs to be updated, `find` works when in a bind, but powerful and cryptic and *can break things.*" Lets continue and begin with the explanations:

1. As mentioned previously, the `locate` command is a relatively simple search tool that uses a database as a backend, which contains an indexed list of all of the files for quick and efficient searches. Locate is not real-time unlike the `find` command, which searches everything as it exists at the time of execution (depending on the parameters provided to find). Locating `stdio.h` will produce several results depending on your system. However, when we run locate again, it does not know or contain any information regarding the `/usr/filethatlocatedoesntknow.txt` and `/usr/filethatlocatedoesntknow2.txt` files. Running `updatedb` will re-index the files and then using the `locate` command will return the appropriate results. Notice that locate works with partial names or full path matching:

```
$ locate stdio.h
/usr/include/stdio.h
/usr/include/c++/5/tr1/stdio.h
/usr/include/x86_64-linux-gnu/bits/stdio.h
/usr/include/x86_64-linux-gnu/unicode/ustdio.h
/usr/lib/x86_64-linux-gnu/perl/5.22.1/CORE/nostdio.h
```

```
/usr/share/man/man7/stdio.h.7posix.gz
$ sudo touch /usr/filethatlocatedoesntknow.txt
/usr/filethatlocatedoesntknow2.txt
$ sudo sh -c 'echo "My dear Watson ol\'boy" >
/usr/filethatlocatedoesntknow.txt'
$ locate filethatlocatedoes
$ sudo updatedb
$ locate filethatlocatedoes
/usr/filethatlocatedoesntknow.txt
/usr/filethatlocatedoesntknow2.txt
```

2. In the second step, we are introduced to some of the amazing functionality provided by the `find` command.

> Again, be aware that using `find` for operations such as deletion can break your system if not handled appropriately or if the input isn't carefully monitored and filtered.

3. At a minimum, the `find` command is executed this way: `$ find ${START_SEARCH_HERE} ${OPTIONAL_PARAMETERS ...}`. In the first use of the find command, we begin searching within our user's home directory (`${HOME}` environment variable), and then use a wild card to look for **hidden files** that begin with a `..`Finally, we use `-ls` to create a file listing. This is not by accident as you may have observed; you can create files that are absent upon first inspection in the GUI's file explorer (especially in your user's home directory) or on the console (for example, unless you use the `ls` command with the `-a` flag). In the next command, we use `find -type d` to search for a directory named `.git`. Then, we search for files that match either `*.sh` or `*.txt` using a special notation for find: `-type f \( -name "*.sh" -o -name "*.txt" \)`. Notice the forward slash `\` and then the parenthesis `(`. We can then specify multiple name matching arguments using `-o -name "string"`.

4. In the third step, we use find to search for subdirectories using `-type d` that are often present inside of cloned or exported git-related directories. We can chain the `find` commands together using this format: `$ cmd 1 && cmd2 && cmd3 && ...`. This guarantees that if the proceeding command evaluates to true, then the next will execute and so on. Then, we introduce the `-exec` flag, which is used to execute another command once a match has been found. In this case, we search for all files and then use grep immediately to search within the file. Notice the `{} +` at the end of the `grep`. This is because `{}` will be replaced with find's returned results. The `+` character delimits the end of the `exec` command, and appends the results so that `rm -rf` will be executed less times than the total number of files found/matched.

5. In the final step, we delete files using two methods. The first method using the `-delete` flag may not be available on all distributions or implementations of find, but upon match, it will delete the file. It is more efficient than executing the sub process `rm` on large numbers of files. Secondly, using `-exec rm -rf {} \;`, we can delete files found easily and in a portable way. However, there is a difference between `\;` and `+` and the difference is that in the `\;` version, `rm -rf` is executed for each file found/matched. Be careful with this command as it is not interactive.

Creating a diff of two files and patching

In what case should you know what a diff is? Or a patch? In the Linux world, it is a way to determine the differences between files and also to solve problems at the OS level (especially if you have a broken driver in the Linux kernel). However, for the purposes of a cookbook, diffs and patches useful for a couple of main things:

- When determining whether a particular script or configuration file has modifications
- When plotting differences between versions, or migrating data between an old to new script, and so on

So, what is a **diff** or **differential**? A diff is the output that describes the differences between two files (file A and file B). The file A is the source, and the B file is the assumed to be modified file. If no diff output is created, then A and B are either empty or there are no differences. Diffs in a unified format typically look like this:

```
$ diff -urN fileA.txt fileB.txt
--- fileA.txt 2017-12-11 15:06:49.972849620 -0500
+++ fileB.txt 2017-12-11 15:08:09.201177398 -0500
@@ -1,3 +1,4 @@
```

```
 12345
-abcdef
+abcZZZ
+789aaa
```

There are several formats of diffs, but the unified format is among the most popular (and used by the FOSS crowd). It contains information about both files (A and B), the line numbers and counts in each, and the content added or changed. If we look at the preceding sample, we can see that in the original, the string abcdef is removed (−) and then re-added (+) as abcdZZZ. And there is the further addition of a new line containing 789aaa (which can also be seen here: @@ −1,3 +1,4 @@).

A patch is a unified diff that contains changes to one or more files that are to be applied in a specific order or method, hence the concept of patching being the process of applying a patch (which contains diff information). A patch can consist of several diffs concatenated together as well.

Getting ready

Besides having a terminal open, these two utilities need to be installed:

```
$ sudo apt-get install patch diff
```

Next, let's create a fake configuration file that's copied from a real one:

```
$ cp /etc/updatedb.conf ~/updatedb-v2.conf
```

Open updatedb-v2.conf and change the contents to look like this:

```
PRUNE_BIND_MOUNTS="yes"
# PRUNENAMES=".git .bzr .hg .svn"
PRUNEPATHS="/tmp /var/spool /media /home/.ecryptfs /var/lib/schroot /media
/mount"
PRUNEFS="NFS nfs nfs4 rpc_pipefs afs binfmt_misc proc smbfs autofs iso9660
ncpfs coda devpts ftpfs devfs mfs shfs sysfs cifs lustre tmpfs usbfs udf
fuse.glusterfs fuse.sshfs curlftpfs ecryptfs fusesmb devtmpfs"
```

In the event that your updatedb-v2.conf looks drastically different, add /media /mount to the PRUNEPATHS variable. Notice that they are separated by a space.

How to do it...

1. Open a terminal, and run the following commands in order to understand the `diff` command:

```
$ diff /etc/updatedb.conf ~/updatedb-v2.conf
$ diff -urN /etc/updatedb.conf ~/updatedb-v2.conf
```

2. At this point, only the diff information has been output to the console's standard out and a patch file has not been created. To create the actual patch file, execute the following command:

```
$ diff -urN /etc/updatedb.conf ~/updatedb-v2.conf > 001-myfirst-
patch-for-updatedb.patch
```

 Patches can be found in many forms, but they usually have the `.patch` extension and are preceded by a number and a human readable name.

3. Now, before applying a patch, it can also be tested to ensure that the results are as expected. Try the following commands:

```
$ echo "NEW LINE" > ~/updatedb-v3.conf
$ cat ~/updatedb-v2.conf >> ~/updatedb-v3.conf
$ patch --verbose /etc/updatedb.conf < 001-myfirst-patch-for-
updatedb.patch
```

4. Let's see what happens when patches fail to apply using the following commands:

```
$ patch --verbose --dry-run ~/updatedb-v1.conf < 001-myfirst-patch-
for-updatedb.patch
$ patch --verbose ~/fileA.txt < 001-myfirst-patch-for-
updatedb.patch
```

How it works...

Repeat after me—*"locate is simple and needs to be updated, find works when in a bind, but powerful and cryptic and can break things."* Let's continue and begin with the explanations:

1. The first `diff` command outputs the changes in the simple diff format. However, in the second instance when running the diff command, we use the `-urN` flag(s). `-u` stands for unified format, `-r` stands for recursive, and `-N` stands for a new file:

```
$ diff /etc/updatedb.conf ~/updatedb-v2.conf
3c3
< PRUNEPATHS="/tmp /var/spool /media /home/.ecryptfs
/var/lib/schroot"
---
> PRUNEPATHS="/tmp /var/spool /media /home/.ecryptfs
/var/lib/schroot /media /mount"
$ diff -urN /etc/updatedb.conf ~/updatedb-v2.conf
--- /etc/updatedb.conf 2014-11-18 02:54:29.000000000 -0500
+++ /home/rbrash/updatedb-v2.conf 2017-12-11 15:26:33.172955754
-0500
@@ -1,4 +1,4 @@
 PRUNE_BIND_MOUNTS="yes"
 # PRUNENAMES=".git .bzr .hg .svn"
-PRUNEPATHS="/tmp /var/spool /media /home/.ecryptfs
/var/lib/schroot"
+PRUNEPATHS="/tmp /var/spool /media /home/.ecryptfs
/var/lib/schroot /media /mount"
 PRUNEFS="NFS nfs nfs4 rpc_pipefs afs binfmt_misc proc smbfs autofs
iso9660 ncpfs coda devpts ftpfs devfs mfs shfs sysfs cifs lustre
tmpfs usbfs udf fuse.glusterfs fuse.sshfs curlftpfs ecryptfs
fusesmb devtmpfs"
```

2. Now, we have created a patch by redirecting standard out to the `001-myfirst-patch-for-updatedb.patch` file:

```
$ diff -urN /etc/updatedb.conf ~/updatedb-v2.conf > 001-myfirst-
patch-for-updatedb.patch
```

3. Now that we have created a modified version of ~/updatedb-v3, notice anything from the dry-run? Ignoring that /etc/updatedb.conf only has read-only permissions (we are just using it for the sake of example as dry-run doesn't alter the contents anyway), we can see that HUNK #1 is applied successfully. A **hunk** stands for a section of the diff, and you can have several for one file or many files inside of the same patch. Did you notice that the line numbers didn't match exactly as those in the patch? It still applied the patch as it knew enough information and **fudged** the data to match so that it would apply successfully. Be aware of this functionality when dealing with large files, which may have similar match criteria:

```
$ patch --verbose --dry-run /etc/updatedb.conf < 001-myfirst-patch-
for-updatedb.patch
Hmm... Looks like a unified diff to me...
The text leading up to this was:
--------------------------
|--- /etc/updatedb.conf 2014-11-18 02:54:29.000000000 -0500
|+++ /home/rbrash/updatedb-v2.conf 2017-12-11 15:26:33.172955754
-0500
--------------------------
File /etc/updatedb.conf is read-only; trying to patch anyway
checking file /etc/updatedb.conf
Using Plan A...
Hunk #1 succeeded at 1.
done
```

4. If we attempt to apply the patch to a file on a file that does not match, it will fail, like in the following output (if --dry-run is specified). If --dry-run is not specified, the failure will be stored in a reject file as is noted in this line: 1 out of 1 hunk FAILED -- saving rejects to file /home/rbrash/fileA.txt.rej:

```
$ patch --verbose --dry-run /etc/updatedb.conf1 < 001-myfirst-
patch-for-updatedb.patch
Hmm... Looks like a unified diff to me...
The text leading up to this was:
--------------------------
|--- /etc/updatedb.conf 2014-11-18 02:54:29.000000000 -0500
|+++ /home/rbrash/updatedb-v2.conf 2017-12-11 15:26:33.172955754
-0500
--------------------------
checking file /etc/updatedb.conf1
Using Plan A...
Hunk #1 FAILED at 1.
1 out of 1 hunk FAILED
done
```

```
$
$ patch --verbose ~/fileA.txt < 001-myfirst-patch-for-
updatedb.patch
Hmm... Looks like a unified diff to me...
The text leading up to this was:
--------------------------
|--- /etc/updatedb.conf 2014-11-18 02:54:29.000000000 -0500
|+++ /home/rbrash/updatedb-v2.conf 2017-12-11 15:26:33.172955754
-0500
--------------------------
patching file /home/rbrash/fileA.txt
Using Plan A...
Hunk #1 FAILED at 1.
1 out of 1 hunk FAILED -- saving rejects to file
/home/rbrash/fileA.txt.rej
done
```

Creating symbolic links and using them effectively

Symbolic links mean shortcuts, right? Well, if you ever heard that explanation, it is only partially correct and they are present on most modern OS. In fact, there are two kinds of symbolic links when thinking in terms of files: hard and soft:

Hard Links	Soft Links
Only link to files	Can link to directories and files
Link to contents on same disk	Can reference files/folders across disks or networks
Reference inode/physical locations	If the original file is deleted, the hard link will remain (in own inodes)
Moving a file will still allow the link to work	Links don't follow the reference file if moved

A soft link will most likely match your expectations of a shortcut and the behavior might not be very surprising, but what use is a hard link? One of the most prominent cases of when to use a hard link is when you don't want to break a link by moving the file it points to! A soft link is clearly more flexible and can work across file systems, which is unlike hard links, but soft links won't work if a file is moved.

Besides creating shortcuts, you can do neat tricks like renaming argv[0] when using symbolic links. The Busybox shell is an example of that, where it contains **applets** that are executed by a symlink that points to ./busybox. For example, ls points to the same binary as cd! All of them point to ./busybox. This is a neat way to save space and improve runtime flags without the use of flags.

Soft links are also used in the /usr/lib or /lib folders for shared librarys. In fact, symlinks are very useful for aliasing paths or getting software to work with hard-coded paths that are inside of the binaries themselves.

How to do it...

1. Open a terminal, and create the whoami.sh script:

```
#!/bin/bash
VAR=$0
echo "I was ran as: $VAR"
```

2. Execute whoami.sh and observe what has happened:

```
$ bash whoami.sh
```

3. Next, create a soft link to whoami.sh using the ln command:

```
$ ln -s whoami.sh ghosts-there-be.sh
```

4. Next, run ls -la. Notice any differences?

```
ls -la ghosts-there-be.sh whoami.sh
```

5. On to hard links, which are created this way using ln:

```
$ ln ghosts-there-be.sh gentle-ghosts-there-be.sh
$ ln whoami.sh real-ghosts-there-be.sh
```

6. Next, let's look at the difference in results when running the commands:

```
$ ls -la ghosts-there-be.sh whoami.sh real-ghosts-there-be.sh
gentle-ghosts-there-be.sh
lrwxrwxrwx 1 rbrash rbrash 18 Dec 12 15:07 gentle-ghosts-there-
be.sh -> ghosts-there-be.sh
lrwxrwxrwx 1 rbrash rbrash 9 Dec 12 14:57 ghosts-there-be.sh ->
```

```
whoami.sh
-rw-rw-r-- 2 rbrash rbrash 45 Dec 12 14:56 real-ghosts-there-be.sh
-rw-rw-r-- 2 rbrash rbrash 45 Dec 12 14:56 whoami.sh
$ mv whoami.sh nobody.sh
$ bash ghosts-there-be.sh
bash: ghosts-there-be.sh: No such file or directory
$ bash real-ghosts-there-be.sh
I was ran as: real-ghosts-there-be.sh
$ bash gentle-ghosts-there-be.sh
bash: gentle-ghosts-there-be.sh: No such file or directory
```

How it works...

In step one, we created `whoami.sh`. It is similar to the `whoami` command, but different because we do not print the `$USER` variable, but rather argument 0 (`arg0`, as its typically known) or `$0`. In laymen's terms, we are printing out the name used to execute the code or script.

When we execute `whoami.sh`, it prints to the console:

```
$ bash whoami.sh
I was ran as: whoami.sh
```

To create a symbolic soft link, we use `ln` with the `-s` flag (for symbolic mode). The `ln` command expects to be executed in this way: `$ ln -s originalFileToBeLinkedTo newFileToLinkToOldFile`.

As we can see in the following code, executing `ghosts-there-be.sh` runs the code in `whoami.sh`, but `arg0` is `ghosts-there-be.sh`. Then, when the `ls` command is ran with the `-l -a` flags (`-la`), we can see the soft link to `whoami.sh`. Notice the small size of 9 bytes!

```
$ bash ghosts-there-be.sh
I was ran as: ghosts-there-be.sh
$ ls -la ghosts-there-be.sh whoami.sh
lrwxrwxrwx 1 rbrash rbrash 9 Dec 12 14:57 ghosts-there-be.sh ->
whoami.sh
-rw-rw-r-- 1 rbrash rbrash 45 Dec 12 14:56 whoami.sh
```

Next, we create a hard link by using the `ls` command without the `-s` flag.

The hard link, `real-ghosts-there-be.sh`, runs the same content as `ghosts-there-be.sh`, but points to the actual contents of `whoami.sh`, even if it is moved and renamed as `nobody.sh`:

```
$ ls -la ghosts-there-be.sh whoami.sh real-ghosts-there-be.sh
gentle-ghosts-there-be.sh
lrwxrwxrwx 1 rbrash rbrash 18 Dec 12 15:07 gentle-ghosts-there-
be.sh -> ghosts-there-be.sh
lrwxrwxrwx 1 rbrash rbrash 9 Dec 12 14:57 ghosts-there-be.sh ->
whoami.sh
-rw-rw-r-- 2 rbrash rbrash 45 Dec 12 14:56 real-ghosts-there-be.sh
-rw-rw-r-- 2 rbrash rbrash 45 Dec 12 14:56 whoami.sh
 mv whoami.sh nobody.sh
$ bash ghosts-there-be.sh
bash: ghosts-there-be.sh: No such file or directory
$ bash real-ghosts-there-be.sh
I was ran as: real-ghosts-there-be.sh
$ bash gentle-ghosts-there-be.sh
bash: gentle-ghosts-there-be.sh: No such file or directory
$ bash gentle-ghosts-there-be.sh
bash: gentle-ghosts-there-be.sh: No such file or directory
```

Crawling filesystem directories and printing a tree

At this point, we already know about the commands locate, find, and grep (plus regular expressions), but what about if we wanted to create our own naive implementation of a directory crawler/scraper/indexer? It certainly won't be the fastest or have optimizations, but we can use recursive functionality and file tests to print a tree-like structure.

 This exercise is a bit of a fun exercise and certainly recreates the proverbial "wheel". This can be easily done by running the tree command, however, this will be useful in an upcoming exercise when we'll be building arrays of arrays for files.

Getting ready

Besides having a terminal open, let's create some test data:

```
$ mkdir -p parentdir/child_with_kids
$ mkdir -p parentdir/second_child_with_kids
$ mkdir -p parentdir/child_with_kids/grand_kid/
```

```
$ touch parentdir/child.txt parentdir/child_with_kids/child.txt
parentdir/child_with_kids/grand_kid/gkid1.txt
$ touch parentdir/second_child_with_kids/cousin1.txt parentdir/z_child.txt
parentdir/child.txt parentdir/child2.txt
```

How to do it...

1. Open a terminal and create the `mytree.sh` script:

```bash
#!/bin/bash
CURRENT_LVL=0

function tab_creator() {
  local X=0
  local LVL=$1
  local TABS="."
  while [ $X -lt $LVL ]
  do
    # Concatonate strings
    TABS="${TABS}${TABS}"
    X=$[$X+1]
  done
  echo -en "$TABS"
}
function recursive_tree() {

  local ENTRY=$1
  for LEAF in ${ENTRY}/*
  do
    if [ -d $LEAF ];then
      # If LEAF is a directory & not empty
      TABS=$(tab_creator $CURRENT_LVL)
      printf "%s\_ %s\n" "$TABS" "$LEAF"
      CURRENT_LVL=$(( CURRENT_LVL + 1 ))
      recursive_tree $LEAF $CURRENT_LVL
      CURRENT_LVL=$(( CURRENT_LVL - 1 ))
    elif [ -f $LEAF ];then
      # Print only the bar and not the backwards slash
      # And only if a file
      TABS=$(tab_creator $CURRENT_LVL)
      printf "%s|_%s\n" "$TABS" "$LEAF"
      continue
    fi
  done
}
```

```
PARENTDIR=$1
recursive_tree $PARENTDIR 1
```

2. In your terminal, now run:

```
$ bash mytree.sh parentdir
```

How it works...

The creation of `mytree.sh` is a trivial task, but the logic inside follows recursive functions. There is also the concept of `${CURRENT_LVL}`, which is used to produce the number of periods (or levels) deep the script is from its original starting point: **parentdir**. In each directory, we create a for loop to test each file/directory inside of it. The logic tests whether the entry is either a file or a director. If it is a directory, we increment `${CURRENT_LVL}` and then **recursively** execute the **same** logic inside of the `recursive_tree` function until done and then return. If the logic is a file, we merely print out and **continue**. The `tab_creator` function makes the variable string for the periods based on `${CURRENT_LVL}` and concatenation.

Executing the script should produce an output similar to the following, but notice how the script remembers how many layers deep it might be, and that the directories are shown with a _ instead of |_:

```
$ bash mytree.sh parentdir
.|_parentdir/child2.txt
.|_parentdir/child.txt
.\_ parentdir/child_with_kids
..|_parentdir/child_with_kids/child.txt
..\_ parentdir/child_with_kids/grand_kid
....|_parentdir/child_with_kids/grand_kid/gkid1.txt
.\_ parentdir/empty_dir
.\_ parentdir/second_child_with_kids
..|_parentdir/second_child_with_kids/cousin1.txt
.|_parentdir/z_child.txt
```

Finding and deleting duplicate files or directories

At one point, we had already talked about checking to see if strings inside of a file were unique and if we could sort them, but we haven't yet performed a similar operation on files. However, before diving in, let's make some assumptions about what constitutes a duplicate file for the purpose of this recipe: a duplicate file is one that may have a different name, but the same contents as another.

One way to investigate the contents of a file would be to remove all white space and purely check the strings contained within, or we could merely use tools such as **SHA512sum** and **MD5sum** to generate a unique hash (think unique string full of gibberish) of the contents of the files. The general flow would be as follows:

1. Using this hash, we can compare the hash against a list of hashes already computed.
2. If the has matches, we have seen the contents of this file before and so we can delete it.
3. If the hash is new, we can record the entry and move onto calculating the hash of the next file until all files have been *hashed*.

> Using a hash does not require you to know how the mathematics work, but rather to be aware of how it's supposed to work IF it is a secure implementation and has enough possibilities to make finding a duplicate computationally unfeasible. Hashes are supposed to be one way, which means that they are different from encryption/decryption so that once a hash has been created, it should be impossible to determine the original input from the hash itself.
> MD5sums are considered completely insecure (although useful where security may be less needed), and SHA1/2 are considered to be potentially on their way out of popularity with the use of SPONGE algorithms in SHA3 (use SHA3 where possible). For more information, please see the NIST guidelines.

Getting ready

Open a terminal and create a data set consisting of several files with the `dsetmkr.sh` script:

```
$ #!/bin/bash
BDIR="files_galore"
```

```
rm -rf ${BDIR}
mkdir -p ${BDIR}

touch $BDIR/file1; echo "11111111111111111111111111111111" > $BDIR/file1;
touch $BDIR/file2; echo "22222222222222222222222222222222" > $BDIR/file2;
touch $BDIR/file3; echo "33333333333333333333333333333333" > $BDIR/file3;
touch $BDIR/file4; echo "44444444444444444444444444444444" > $BDIR/file4;
touch $BDIR/file5; echo "44444444444444444444444444444444" > $BDIR/file5;
touch $BDIR/sameas5; echo "44444444444444444444444444444444" >
$BDIR/sameas5;
touch $BDIR/sameas1; echo "11111111111111111111111111111111" >
$BDIR/sameas1;
```

Then, before jumping into scripting, a core concept needs to be discussed regarding arrays and whether they are static or dynamic; knowing how an array implementation works at its core is a key principle if performance is an objective.

Arrays can be really helpful, but the performance of a Bash script is often sub-par to that of a compiled program or even choosing a language with the appropriate data structures. In Bash, arrays are linked lists and dynamic, which means that if you resize the array, there isn't a massive performance penalty.

For our purposes, we are going to create a dynamic array and once the array becomes quite large, it will be the searching of the array which becomes the performance bottleneck. This naive iterative approach usually works well up to an arbitrary amount (let's say, N), and at which the benefits of using another mechanism may outweigh the simplicity of the current approach. For those who want to know more about data structures and the performance of them, check out Big O notation and complexity theory.

How to do it...

1. Open a terminal, and create the `file-deduplicator.sh` script.

   The following is a code snippet of the script:

   ```
   #!/bin/bash

   declare -a FILE_ARRAY=()

   function add_file() {
     # echo $2 $1
     local NUM_OR_ELEMENTS=${#FILE_ARRAY[@]}
     FILE_ARRAY[$NUM_OR_ELEMENTS+1]=$1
   }
   ```

```
function del_file() {
  rm "$1" 2>/dev/null
}
```

2. Run the `setup` command if not already: run $ `bash dsetmkr.sh` and then run $ `bash ./file-deduplicator.sh`. Enter `files_galore/` at the prompt and press *Enter*:

```
$ bash dsetmkr.sh
$ bash file-deduplicator.sh
Enter directory name to being searching and deduplicating:
Press [ENTER] when ready

files_galore/
#1
f559f33eee087ea5ac75b2639332e97512f305fc646cf422675927d4147500d4c4a
a573bd3585bb866799d08c373c0427ece87b60a5c42dbee9c011640e04d75
#2
f7559990a03f2479bf49c85cb215daf60417cb59875b875a8a517c069716eb9417d
fdb907e50c0fd5bd47127105b7df9e68a0c45a907dc5254ce6bc64d7ec82a
#3
2811ce292f38147613a84fdb406ef921929f864a627f78ef0ef16271d4996ed598d
0f5c5f410f7ae75f9902ff0f63126b567e5f24882db3686be81f2a79f1bb3
#4
89f5df2b9f4908adca6a36f92b344d4a8ff96d04184e99d8dd31a86e96d45a1aa16
a8b574d5815f17d649d521c9472670441a56f54dc1c2640e20567581d9b4e
```

3. Review the results and verify the contents of `files_galore`.

```
$ ls files_galore/
```

How it works...

Before getting started, a proceeding note of caution: the `file-deduplicator.sh` script deletes duplicate files in the directory it is targeted at.

1. Getting started (especially using the `dsetmkr.sh` script), we will produce a directory called `files_galore` that also contains several files: four are unique and three contain duplicate content:

```
$ bash dsetmkr.sh
```

The study of cryptography, security, and mathematics are all very interesting and broad information domains! Hashes have a multitude of other uses such as integrity checking of files, lookup values to find data quickly, unique identifiers, and much more.

2. When you run `file-deduplicator.sh`, it begins by asking the user for input using `read` and then it prints out four different values with seemingly random strings of characters. *Random* looking is absolutely correct—they are SHA512 hash sums! Each string is the sum of the contents inside of it. Even if the contents are even slightly different (for example, one bit has been flipped to a `1` instead of a `0`), then a totally different hash sum will be produced. Again, this bash script leverages a foreign concept of arrays (using a global array variable meaning accessible everywhere in the script) and hash sums using the **SHA512sum** tool combined with **awk** to retrieve the correct values. This script is not recursive though, and only looks at the files inside of `files_galore` to generate a list of files, a hash for each one, and search an array containing all *known* hashes. If a hash is unknown, then it is a new file and is inserted into the array for storage. Otherwise, if a hash is seen twice, the file is deleted because it contains DUPLICATE content (even if the file name is different). There is another aspect here, and that is the use of return values as strings. As you may remember, return only can return numeric values:

```
$ bash file-deduplicator.sh
Enter directory name to being searching and deduplicating:
Press [ENTER] when ready

files_galore/
#1
f559f33eee087ea5ac75b2639332e97512f305fc646cf422675927d4147500d4c4a
a573bd3585bb866799d08c373c0427ece87b60a5c42dbee9c011640e04d75
#2
f7559990a03f2479bf49c85cb215daf60417cb59875b875a8a517c069716eb9417d
fdb907e50c0fd5bd47127105b7df9e68a0c45a907dc5254ce6bc64d7ec82a
#3
2811ce292f38147613a84fdb406ef921929f864a627f78ef0ef16271d4996ed598d
0f5c5f410f7ae75f9902ff0f63126b567e5f24882db3686be81f2a79f1bb3
#4
89f5df2b9f4908adca6a36f92b344d4a8ff96d04184e99d8dd31a86e96d45a1aa16
a8b574d5815f17d649d521c9472670441a56f54dc1c2640e20567581d9b4e
```

3. After executing the operation, we can see that the `files_galore` directory only contains four files out of the original seven. The duplicate data is now removed!

```
$ ls files_galore/
file1 file2 file3 file4
```

Joining and splitting files at arbitrary positions

Let's not be shy! Who has tried to open a large file by accident or even intentionally with an application and it didn't quite go as planned? I certainly have, and I have certainly seen the limitations such as the number of rows loaded in Excel, or OpenOffice calculator. In these cases, we use a handy tool that can split files at arbitrary points, such as the following:

- Before X number of lines
- Before Z number of bytes/chars

In this recipe, you will create a singe dual purpose script: a script that can use an input file and produce *split* or multiple files, and a second script to join files using a combining method. There are a few caveats when passing around string variables as they:

- Can sometimes lose special characters such as new lines
- (Binary) Should be handled by different tools than the usual commands on the command line

This file also reuses the `getopts` parameter parsing we saw earlier in Chapter 1, *Crash Course in Bash*, but it also introduces the `mktemp` command and the `getconf` command with the `PAGESIZE` parameter. `Mktemp` is a useful command because it can produce unique temporary files that reside in the `/tmp` directory, but can even produce unique files that follow a template (notice the XXX—this will be replaced with random values, but `uniquefile.` will remain):

```
$ mktemp uniquefile.XXXX
```

Another useful command is the `getconf` programming utility, which is a standards compliant tool designed to fetch useful system variables. One in particular called `PAGESIZE` is useful to determine the size of memory in one block. Obviously, this is in very simplistic terms, but choosing the appropriate size to write data can be very beneficial performance-wise.

Getting ready

Besides having a terminal open, a single text file called `input-lines` needs to be created with the following content (one character on each line):

```
1
2
3
4
5
6
7
8
9
0
a
b
c
d
e
f
g
h
i
j
k
```

Next, create a second file called `merge-lines` with the following content:

```
It's -17 outside
```

How to do it...

Open a terminal and create a script named `file-splitter.sh`.

The following is the code snippet:

```
#!/bin/bash
FNAME=""
LEN=10
TYPE="line"
OPT_ERROR=0
set -f

function determine_type_of_file() {
  local FILE="$1"
```

```
      file -b "${FILE}" | grep "ASCII text" > /dev/null
      RES=$?
      if [ $RES -eq 0 ]; then
        echo "ASCII file - continuing"
      else
        echo "Not an ASCII file, perhaps it is Binary?"
      fi
    }
```

Next, run `file-splitter.sh` with this command and flags (`-i`, `-t`, `-l`):

```
$ bash file-splitter.sh -i input-lines -t line -l 10
```

Review the output and see what the difference is with `-t size` and when `-l line` is used. What about when `-l 1` or `-l 100` is used? Remember to remove the split files using `$ rm input-lines.*`:

```
$ rm input-lines.*
$ bash file-splitter.sh -i input-lines -t line -l 10
$ rm input-lines.*
$ bash file-splitter.sh -i input-lines -t line -l 1
$ rm input-lines.*
$ bash file-splitter.sh -i input-lines -t line -l 100
$ rm input-lines.*
$ bash file-splitter.sh -i input-lines -t size -l 10
```

In the next step, create another script called `file-joiner.sh`.

The following is the code snippet:

```
#!/bin/bash
INAME=""
ONAME=""
FNAME=""
WHERE=""
OPT_ERROR=0

TMPFILE1=$(mktemp)

function determine_type_of_file() {
  local FILE="$1"
  file -b "${FILE}" | grep "ASCII text" > /dev/null
  RES=$?
  if [ $RES -eq 0 ]; then
    echo "ASCII file - continuing"
  else
    echo "Not an ASCII file, perhaps it is Binary?"
  fi
```

```
  }
```

Next, run the script using this command:

```
$ bash file-joiner.sh -i input-lines -o merge-lines -f final-
join.txt -w 2
```

How it works...

Before proceeding, notice that the type option (-t) on `final-join.txt` ignores \n newlines when reading in characters one at a time. Read suffices for the purpose of this recipe, but the reader should be aware that read/cat are not the best tools for this type of work.

1. Creating the script was trivial and for the most part shouldn't look like it came from the planet Mars.

2. Running the `$ bash file-splitter.sh -i input-lines -t line -l 10` command should produce three files, all of which are input-lines {1,...,3}. The reason that there is three files is that if you used the same input, which is 22 lines long, it will produce three files (10+10+2). Using read and echo using a concatenated buffer (`${BUFFER}`), we can write to the file based on a specific criteria (provided by -l). If the **EOF** or end of file is met and the done loop is done, we need to write the buffer to the file because it may be under the threshold of the write criteria—this would result in lost/missing bytes in the last file created by the `splitter` script:

```
$ bash file-splitter.sh -i input-lines -t line -l 10
ASCII file - continuing
Wrote buffer to file: input-lines.1
Wrote buffer to file: input-lines.2
Wrote buffer to file: input-lines.3
```

3. Depending on the usage of the -l flag, the value of 1 will produce a file for every line, and the value of 100 will produce a single file because if fits under the threshold. Using the side-feature -t size, which can be used to split based on bytes, read has an unfortunate side effect: when we pass the buffer, it is altered and the new lines are missing. This sort of activity would be better if we used a tool such as dd, which is better for copying, writing, and creating raw data to files or devices.

4. Next, we created the script called `file-joiners.sh`. Again, it used `getopts` and requires four input parameters: `-i originalFile -o, otherFileToMerge -f, finalMergedFile -w,` and `whereInjectTheOtherFile`. The script is simpler overall, but uses the `mktemp` command to create a temporary file which we can use as a storage buffer without modifying the originals. When we are finished, we can use the `mv` command to move the file from `/tmp` to the terminal's current directory (`.`). The `mv` command can also be used to rename files and is usually faster than `cp` (not so much in this case) because a copy does not occur, rather just a renaming operation at the file system level.

5. Catting `final-join.txt` should contain the following output:

```
$ cat final-join.txt
1
2
It's -17 outside
3
4
5
6
7
8
9
0
a
b
c
d
e
f
g
h
i
j
k
```

Generating datasets and random files of various size

Usually, data that mimics real-world data is always the best, but sometimes we need an assortment of files of various content and size for validation testing without delay. Imagine that you have a web server and it is running some sort of application that accepts files for storage. However, the files have a size limit being enforced. Wouldn't it be great to just *whip up* a batch of files in an instant?

To do this, we can use some few file system features such as /dev/random and a useful program called dd. The dd command is a utility that can be used to convert and copy files (including devices due to Linux's concept of everything is a file, more or less). It can be used in a later recipe to back up data on an SD card (remember your favorite Raspberry Pi project?) or to "chomp" through files byte by byte without losses. Typical minimal dd usage can be $ dd if="inputFile" of="outputFile" bs=1M count=10. From this command, we can see:

- if=: Stands for input file
- of=: Stands for output file
- bs=: Stands for block size
- count=: Stands for numbers of blocks to be copied

Options bs= and count= are optional if you want to perform a 1:1 (pure duplicate) copy of a file because dd will attempt to use reasonably efficient parameters to provide adequate performance. The dd command also has a number of other options such as seek=, which will be explored later when performing low-level backups in another recipe. The count option is typically not needed as it's far more common to copy an entire file instead of a section (when performing backups).

 /dev/random is a device in Linux (hence the /dev path) which can be used to produce random numbers for use in your scripts or applications. There are also other /dev paths such as the console and various adaptors (for example, USB sticks or mice), all of which may be accessible, and gaining knowledge of them is recommended.

Getting ready

To get ready for this recipe, install the `dd` command as follows and make a new directory called `qa-data/`:

```
$ sudo apt-get install dd bsdmainutils
$ mkdir qa-data
```

This recipe uses the `dmesg` command, which is used to return system information such as interface status or the system boot process. It is nearly always present on a system and therefore a good substitute to reasonable system level "lorem ipsum". If you wish to use another type of random text, or a dictionary of words, `dmesg` can easily be replaced! Another two commands used are `seq` and `hexdump`. The `seq` command can generate an array of *n* numbers from a starting point using a specified increment, and `hexdump` produces a human readable representation of a binary (or executable) in hexadecimal format.

How to do it...

Open a terminal and create a new script called `data-maker.sh`.

The following is the code snippet of the script:

```
#!/bin/bash

N_FILES=3
TYPE=binary
DIRECTORY="qa-data"
NAME="garbage"
EXT=".bin"
UNIT="M"
RANDOM=$$
TMP_FILE="/tmp/tmp.datamaker.sh"

function get_random_number() {
  SEED=$(($(date +%s%N)/100000))
  RANDOM=$SEED
  # Sleep is needed to make sure that the next time rnadom is ran,
everything is good.
  sleep 3
  local STEP=$1
  local VARIANCE=$2
  local UPPER=$3
  local LOWER=$VARIANCE
```

```
        local ARR;
        INC=0
        for N in $( seq ${LOWER} ${STEP} ${UPPER} );
        do
          ARR[$INC]=$N
          INC=$(($INC+1))
        done
        RAND=$[$RANDOM % ${#ARR[@]}]
        echo $RAND
    }
```

Let's begin the execution of the script using the following command. It uses the −t flag for type and is set to text, −n is used for the number of files, which is 5, −1 is the lower bound: 1 characters, and -u is 1000 characters:

```
$ bash data-maker.sh -t text -n 5 -l 1 -u 1000
```

To checkout the output, use the following command:

```
$ ls -la qa-data/*.txt
$ tail qa-data/garbage4.txt
```

Again, let's run the data-maker.sh script, but for binary files. Instead of the size limits being 1 char (1 byte) or 1000 chars (1000 bytes or just less than one kilobyte), the sizes are in MB, with there being 1-10 MB files:

```
$ bash data-maker.sh -t binary -n 5 -l 1 -u 10
```

To check out the output, use the following command. The use of a new command called hexdump is because we cannot "dump" or "cat" a binary file the same way as we can a "regular" ASCII text file:

```
$ ls -la qa-data/*.bin
$ hexdump qa-data/garbage0.bin
0000000 0000 0000 0000 0000 0000 0000 0000 0000
*
```

How it works...

Let's understand, how things are happening:

1. First, we create the `;data-maker.sh` script. This script introduces several new concepts including the ever fascinating concept of randomization. In computers, or really anything in life, true random events or number generation cannot happen and require several mathematical principles such as entropy. While this is beyond the scope of this cookbook, know that when reusing it randomly or even initially, you should give it a unique initialization vector or seed. Using a for loop, we can build an array of numbers using the `seq` command. Once the array is built, we choose a "random" value from the array. In each type of file output operation (binary or text), we determine approximately both minimum (`-l` or lower) and maximum (`-u` or upper) sizes to control the output data.

2. In step 2, we build 5 text files using the output of `dmesg` and our pseudo randomization process. We can see that we iterate until we have five text files created using different sizes and starting points with the `dd` command.

3. In step 3, we verify that indeed we created five files, and in the fifth one, we viewed the `tail` of the `garbage4.txt` file.

4. In step 4, we create five binary files (full of zeros) using the `dd` command. Instead of using a number of chars, we used megabytes or (MB).

5. In step 5, we verify that indeed we created five binary files, and in the fifth one, we viewed the contents of the binary file using the `hexdump` command. The `hexdump` command created a simplified "dump" of all of the bytes inside of the `garbage0.bin` file.

4
Making a Script Behave Like a Daemon

In this chapter, we will introduce the following topics:

- Running a program continuously (forever) using looping constructs or recursion
- Keeping programs/scripts running after logoff
- Invoking commands when they require permissions
- Sanitizing user input and for repeatable results
- Making a simple multi-level user menu using select
- Generating and trapping signals for cleanup
- Using temporary files and lock files in your program
- Leveraging timeout when waiting for command completion
- Creating a file-in-file-out program and running processes in parallel
- Executing your script on startup

Introduction

This chapter is about creating components that mimic application functionality such as menus or a daemon. For that to happen, let's step back for a second and determine: what defines an application or daemon? Is it menus? Is it the ability to run *forever*? Or the ability to run *headless* in the background? All of this defines behaviors that an application may exhibit, but nothing prevents a script from also having these behaviors as well!

For example, if a bash script did not have an extension (for example, .sh) and was not ran explicitly with the Bash interpreter, how would you know on the first inspection that it was a script and not a binary? While there are a number of ways such as opening, or using the file command, on the surface, a script can appear the same as a program!

Running a program continuously (forever) using looping constructs or recursion

So far, this cookbook has mostly shown scripts that serve a single purpose and exit upon task completion. This is great for single use scripts, but what about if we wanted to have scripts execute multiple scripts through a menu, or perform tasks in the background automatically forever without being executed each time by scheduling processes (like cron)? This recipe introduces a few ways for a script to run forever until it is killed or exits.

Getting ready

Besides having a terminal open, we need to remember a few concepts:

- Recursive functions combined with a prompt (for example, the `read` command) can result in a script that loops based on user input
- Looping constructs such as `for`, `while`, and `until` can be executed in such a way that a condition is never met and cannot exit

Therefore, a loop or something that causes a loop will force a program to run for an indefinite period of time until an exit event occurs.

 In many programming languages, a program will be executed through the concept of a main function. Within this `main` function, often programmers create what's called a run loop, which allows the program to run forever (even if it is doing nothing).

Using the recursive method, the operation may look like this:

1. The script or program enters a recursive function
2. The recursive function can continue calling itself indefinitely, or, wait for a blocking input (for example, the `read` command)
3. Based on the input provided by the `read` command, you could call the same function again
4. Go back to step 1 until exit

Alternatively, the looping mechanism is similar except functions are not necessarily executed. A loop with an effectively unreachable condition will continuously run unless something interrupts the execution (for example, `sleep`).

A loop running continuously without pause will use CPU resources that could be used elsewhere or waste CPU cycles. If you are running on a battery or a resource constrained platform, extra CPU activity is best to be avoided where possible.

 Using the `sleep` command is an excellent way to limit CPU usage when using loops in simple scripts. However, time adds up if you are running a long script!

How to do it...

Let's start our activity as follows:

1. Open a terminal and create the `recursive_read_input.sh` script:

```
#!/bin/bash

function recursive_func() {

    echo -n "Press anything to continue loop "
    read input
    recursive_func
}

recursive_func
exit 0
```

2. Execute the `$ bash recursive_read_input.sh` script—press *Enter* at the prompt and wait for another prompt.
3. Exit the program with *Ctrl* + C.
4. Open a terminal and create the `loop_for_input.sh` script:

```
#!/bin/bash
for (( ; ; ))
do
    echo "Shall run for ever"
    sleep 1
done
exit 0
```

5. Execute the `$ bash loop_for_input.sh` script—press *Enter* at the prompt and wait for another prompt.

6. Exit the program with *Ctrl + C*.
7. Open a terminal and create the `loop_while_input.sh` script:

```bash
#!/bin/bash
EXIT_PLEASE=0
while : # Notice no conditions?
do
    echo "Pres CTRL+C to stop..."
    sleep 1
    if [ $EXIT_PLEASE != 0 ]; then
       break
     fi
done
exit 0
```

8. Execute the `$ bash loop_while_input.sh` script—press *Enter* at the prompt and wait for another prompt.
9. Exit the program with *Ctrl + C*.
10. Open a terminal and create the `loop_until_input.sh` script:

```bash
#!/bin/bash
EXIT_PLEASE=0
until [ $EXIT_PLEASE != 0 ] # EXIT_PLEASE is set to 0, until will
never be satisfied
do
    echo "Pres CTRL+C to stop..."
    sleep 1
done
exit 0
```

11. Execute the `$ bash loop_until_input.sh` script—press *Enter* at the prompt and wait for another prompt.
12. Exit the program with *Ctrl + C*.

How it works...

Let's understand our script in detail:

1. Creating the `recursive_read_input.sh` script is a simple process. We can see that the `read` command expects input (and will store it in the `$input` variable), then the script calls `recursive_func()` again for *each* time a read exits.

2. Executing the script with $ bash recursive_read_input.sh runs the script indefinitely. No matter the input, *Ctrl + C* or killing the script will exit it.

3. Creating the loop_for_input.sh script is relatively trivial as well. We can notice two things: the for loop has no parameters, except for ((; ;)) and the sleep command. This will make it run forever, but upon each execution of the loop, it will echo Shall run for ever to the console and sleep one second before continuing to the next loop.

4. Executing the $ bash loop_for_input.sh script will cause the script to loop forever.

5. *Ctrl + C* will cause the script to exit.

6. Use the loop_while_input.sh script by using a while loop with the : noop command. However, there is a small difference of an if statement (which will never evaluate to true), but it can still be used in another script to set a condition which causes the script to break the while loop and exit.

7. Executing the $ bash loop_while_input.sh script will cause the script to loop forever.

8. *Ctrl + C* will cause the script to exit.

9. The loop_until_input.sh script is similar to the while loop forever example, but it is different because you can also embed a condition, which will never evaluate to true. This causes the script to loop forever unless the $EXIT_PLEASE variable is set to 1.

10. Executing the $ bash loop_until_input.sh script will cause the script to loop forever.

11. *Ctrl + C* will cause the script to exit.

Keeping programs/scripts running after logoff

Leading up to getting our scripts to run as daemons, we need to know how to keep commands running after a user logs off (or better yet, have them started by the system itself (we will look at this in more detail later). When a user logs in, a session for that user is created, but when they log off—unless the system owns it, processes and scripts typically get killed or closed.

This recipe is about keeping your scripts and activities running in the background after you log off.

Getting ready

Besides having a terminal open, we need to remember a few concepts:

- When a user logs off, any apps or processes owned by the current user will exit (the shell will send a signal)
- The shell is configurable to not send a shutdown signal to processes
- Applications and scripts use stdin and stdout for the usual operations
- Applications or scripts in the background can be referred to as **jobs**

The purpose of this chapter is to not show you process management, but how we can manipulate the shell to keep our programs running. One neat way is by using &, which is used this way: $ bash runforver.sh &. Unfortunately, using only this technique, we are back at square one—our binary still dies when we exit. Therefore, we need to use programs such as **screen**, **disown**, and **sighup**.

 The screen command is not available on all systems. It is recommended that we use another command in case **screen** is absent (it is still useful to know!).

How to do it...

Let's start our activity as follows:

1. Open a terminal and create the loop_and_print.sh script:

```
#!/bin/bash
EXIT_PLEASE=0
INC=0

until [ ${EXIT_PLEASE} != 0 ] # EXIT_PLEASE is set to 0, until will
never be satisfied
do
    echo "Boo $INC" > /dev/null
    INC=$((INC + 1))
    sleep 1
done
exit 0
```

2. Open a terminal and run the following commands:

```
$ bash loop_and_print.sh &
```

```
$ ps aux | grep loop_and_print.sh # Take note of the PID - write it
down
```

3. Next, log off, then log in and run the following command in a new terminal:

```
$ ps aux | grep loop_and_print.sh # Take note of the PID - write it
down
```

4. Can you find the process running? Next, run the following command:

```
$ bash loop_and_print.sh & # note the PID againg
$ disown
```

5. Next, log off, then log in and run the following command in a new terminal:

```
$ ps aux | grep loop_and_print.sh # Take note of the PID - write it
down
```

6. Next, run the following command:

```
$ nohup bash loop_and_print.sh &
```

7. Next, log off, then log in and run the following command in a new terminal:

```
$ ps aux | grep loop_and_print.sh # Take note of the PID - write it
down
```

How it works...

1. In step 1, we opened a terminal and created the loop_and_print.sh script. This script merely loops forever, printing as it does.

2. The following commands will use the loop_and_print.sh script and run in the background as a **job**. The ps command outputs process information and is piped through grep to simplify the output. In the command, we can see the process ID (PID) next to the username column. Keep note of PIDs so that you can kill zombie processes or stop unnecessary applications:

```
$ bash loop_and_print.sh &
[1] 4510
$ ps aux | grep loop_and_print.sh # Take note of the PID - write it
down
rbrash 4510 0.0 0.0 12548 3024 pts/2 S 12:58 0:00 bash
loop_and_print.sh
```

3. Logging back on and running the `ps` command will produce *zero* results. This is because the script we put into the background using `&` has been sent a signal to shutdown or die.

4. Again, we run the `loop_and_print.sh` script; command puts it into the *background,* and disown removes the the background process(es) from the known list of jobs. This *disconnects* the script and *all* output from any terminal.

5. Upon logging back in and using the `ps` command, you shall see the PID of the command:

```
rbrash 8097 0.0 0.0 12548 3024 pts/2 S 13:02 0:00 bash
loop_and_print.sh
```

6. The `nohup` command is similar to the `disown` command, except that it explicitly *disconnects* the script from the current shell. It is *also* different from disown because `nohup` allows you still retain output from the script, which is accessible by other applications after the fact in the `nohup.out` file:

```
$ nohup bash loop_and_print.sh &
[2] 14256
$ nohup: ignoring input and appending output to 'nohup.out'
```

7. Upon logging back in and using the `ps` command, you shall see the PIDs of the *two* scripts that survived the logoff:

```
$ ps aux | grep loop_and_print.sh
rbrash 4510 0.0 0.0 12548 3024 pts/2 S 12:58 0:00 bash
loop_and_print.sh
rbrash 14256 0.0 0.0 12548 3024 pts/2 S 13:02 0:00 bash
loop_and_print.sh
```

Invoking commands when they require permissions

Running as root is dangerous, although sometimes convenient—especially when you are new to Linux and password prompts seem to be a hassle. So far, as a Linux user, you may have seen the `sudo` command or the `su` command. These commands can allow a user to change users on the system at the console or execute commands momentarily with higher permissions (if the user has `sudo` permissions). Sudo, or **substitute user do,** enables a regular user to escalate (raise) their user permissions to a more privileged level for a SINGLE command.

Alternatively, the substitute user command, or su, allows you to also run commands that are privileged and to even change shells (for example, to become a root user). Sudo doesn't activate a root shell or allow you access to other user accounts, which is unlike the su command.

Here are some example uses of the two commands:

```
$ sudo ls /root
$ su -c 'ls /root'
$ su -
```

While both commands require knowledge of a root password, sudo also requires that the user executing the sudo command is listed in the /etc/sudoers file:

```
$ sudo /etc/sudoers
[sudo] password for rbrash:
#
# This file MUST be edited with the 'visudo' command as root.
#
# Please consider adding local content in /etc/sudoers.d/ instead of
# directly modifying this file.
#
# See the man page for details on how to write a sudoers file.
#
Defaults env_reset
Defaults mail_badpass
Defaults
secure_path="/usr/local/sbin:/usr/local/bin:/usr/sbin:/usr/bin:/sbin:/bin:/
snap/bin"

# Host alias specification

# User alias specification

# Cmnd alias specification

# User privilege specification
root ALL=(ALL:ALL) ALL

# Members of the admin group may gain root privileges
%admin ALL=(ALL) ALL

# Allow members of group sudo to execute any command
%sudo ALL=(ALL:ALL) ALL

# See sudoers(5) for more information on "#include" directives:
```

```
#includedir /etc/sudoers.d
```

In the preceding standard Ubuntu sudoers file, we can see that the admin group of users can use the `sudo` command (and likely the reason you are able to do so as well without tinkering). We can also see that there can be specific user privilege execution:

```
root ALL=(ALL:ALL) ALL
```

This indicates that the root user can run all the commands available on the system. In fact, we could add a line for a user named `rbrash`, such as `rbrash ALL=(ALL) ALL`.

`/etc/sudoers` can be edited by a user with root permissions using the `visudo` command:

```
$ sudo visudo
```

 Be careful when adding permissions or alterations to users. It could become a security risk if the account is not secure!

At the end of the day, you might wonder why this is so important for a Bash script (besides being able to escalate permissions). Well, imagine that you might have a system in place that performs Continuous Integration or a process that builds software continuously (for example, Jenkins)—it might just be desirable to have a build running various commands without your input, hence the use of giving a user access to specific commands (especially if they are **sandboxed** or within a **virtual machine**).

Getting ready

Besides having a terminal open, we need to remember a few concepts:

- `sudo` requires a password (unless specified)
- `sudo` can also be limited to specific commands, users, or hosts
- `sudo` commands are also logged in either
  `/var/log/secure` or `/var/log/auth.log`:

  ```
  Dec 23 16:16:19 moon sudo:  rbrash : TTY=pts/2 ;
  PWD=/home/rbrash/Desktop/book ; USER=root ; COMMAND=/usr/bin/vi
  /var/log/auth.log
  Dec 23 16:16:19 moon sudo: pam_unix(sudo:session): session opened
  for user root by (uid=0)
  ```

Additionally, we can create a new user for this recipe:

```
$ sudo useradd bob
$ sudo passwd bob #use password
```

How to do it...

Let's start our activity as follows:

1. Run the command in a new terminal, *not* as `root`, and without any previous `sudo` authorization:

   ```
   $ shutdown -h 10
   $ shutdown -c
   ```

2. Now, execute the `$ sudo visudo` command and edit the script to include the following lines:

   ```
   $ sudo visudo
   [sudo] password for rbrash:
   #
   Defaults env_reset
   Defaults mail_badpass
   Defaults
   secure_path="/usr/local/sbin:/usr/local/bin:/usr/sbin:/usr/bin:/sbi
   n:/bin:/snap/bin"

   # Host alias specification

   # User alias specification

   # Cmnd alias specification

   Cmnd_Alias READ_CMDS = /sbin/halt, /sbin/shutdown

   # User privilege specification
   root ALL=(ALL:ALL) ALL

   bob ALL=(ALL:ALL) NOPASSWD: READ_CMDS

   # Members of the admin group may gain root privileges
   %admin ALL=(ALL) ALL

   # Allow members of group sudo to execute any command
   %sudo ALL=(ALL:ALL) ALL
   ```

```
# See sudoers(5) for more information on "#include" directives:

#includedir /etc/sudoers.d
```

3. Run the command in a new terminal, *not* as `root` and without any previous `sudo` authorization:

```
$ shutdown -h 10
$ shutdown -c
```

4. Notice anything different? Now, make sure to cancel the shutdown using the previous command: `$ shutdown -c`.

How it works...

The preceding recipe is pretty slim, but there is a fair bit of assumption and knowledge that you need to know about in regards to `sudo`. First, be careful. Second, be more careful. And finally, take care to keep your account secure with adequate password policies:

1. In step one, we tried to run two commands that require user permissions. Normally, rebooting or halting a system requires privilege escalation (unless done through the GUI). The `shutdown -c` command cancels a shutdown. If you used `shutdown -h` now, the system would shut down immediately. This cannot be stopped.
2. In the second step, we use the new `visudo` command to make edits to the `/etc/sudoers` file. In bold, `Cmnd_Alias` allows you define a group of commands, however, you have to use the full path of binaries. The user Bob is assigned to this Alias as well. `NOPASSWD:` is used to specify that the password is not required for these commands
3. In the third step, shutdown commands can be run without a password prompt.
4. The final step is to guarantee an accidental shutdown is cancelled.

Sanitizing user input and for repeatable results

One of the best practices for scripts (or programs, for that matter) is controlling user input, not only for security, but for controlling functionality in a way that input provides predictable results. For example, imagine a user who enters a number instead of a string. Did you check it? Will it cause your script to exit prematurely? Or will an unforeseen event occur such as the user entering `rm -rf /*` instead of a valid user name?

In any case, limiting program user input is also useful to you as the author because it can limit paths users take and reduce undefined behavior or bugs. Therefore, if quality assurance is important, test cases and input/output validation can be reduced.

Getting ready

This recipe might be introducing some readers to a concept they would like to avoid: software engineering. It's true, you are probably writing scripts to quickly get a task completed, but if your script is to be used by other people (or for a long time), its great to catch errors early when they occur and prevent program misbehaviour.

 Even without formal computer science or engineering training, the idea of use cases is based on having any particular piece of functionality, with X input, and seeing whether Y does as expected. Sometimes, limits or ranges can be imposed, an action may complete or fail, and any results compared can conclude whether the "use case" passes or fails.

Let's look at a step by step example using a program that should `echo` the username of the user who executed the script via a prompt:

1. The script expects input to be read into a variable using the read command (for example).
2. The variable is assumed to be a string, but it could be the user's name, a number, a post address in a foreign country, an email, or even a malicious command.
3. The script reads the variable and runs the `echo` command.
4. The results returned could be garbage, but could also be executed by another script—what could go wrong?

For example, usernames, by default, should contain alphabetic characters and numbers, but no special characters except underscores, periods, dashes, and a dollar sign ($) at the *end* of a name.

In all efforts, if security is not important, then the robustness of an application could be!

How to do it...

Let's start our activity as follows:

1. Begin by opening a terminal and a new shell script called `bad_input.sh` with the following contents:

```
#!/bin/bash

FILE_NAME=$1
echo $FILE_NAME
ls $FILE_NAME
```

2. Now, run the following commands:

```
$ touch TEST.txt
$ mkdir new_dir/
$ bash bad_input.sh "."
$ bash bad_input.sh "../"
```

3. Create a second script called `better_input.sh`:

```
#!/bin/bash
FILE_NAME=$1

# first, strip underscores
FILE_NAME_CLEAN=${FILE_NAME//_/}

FILE_NAME_CLEAN=$(sed 's/..//g' <<< ${FILE_NAME_CLEAN})

# next, replace spaces with underscores
FILE_NAME_CLEAN=${FILE_NAME_CLEAN// /_}

# now, clean out anything that's not alphanumeric or an underscore
FILE_NAME_CLEAN=${FILE_NAME_CLEAN//[^a-zA-Z0-9_.]/}

# here you should check to see if the file exists before running
the command
ls "${FILE_NAME_CLEAN}"
```

4. Next, run the script using these commands and not the output:

```
$ bash better_input.sh "."
$ bash better_input.sh "../"
$ bash better_input.sh "anyfile"
```

5. Next, create a new script called `validate_email.sh` to validate email addresses (similarly to how one would validate DNS names):

```
#!/bin/bash

EMAIL=$1
echo "${EMAIL}" | grep '^[a-zA-Z0-9._]*@[a-zA-Z0-9]*\.[a-zA-Z0-9]*
RES=$?
if [ $RES -ne 1 ]; then
    echo "${EMAIL} is valid"
else
    echo "${EMAIL} is NOT valid"
fi >/dev/null
RES=$?
if [ $RES -ne 1 ]; then
    echo "${EMAIL} is valid"
else
    echo "${EMAIL} is NOT valid"
fi
```

6. Again, we can test the output:

```
$ bash validate_email.sh ron.brash@somedomain.com
ron.brash@somedomain.com is valid
$ bash validate_email.sh ron.brashsomedomain.com
ron.brashsomedomain.com is NOT valid
```

7. Another common task would be to validate IP addresses. Create another script called `validate_ip.sh` with the following contents:

```
#!/bin/bash

IP_ADDR=$1
IFS=.
if echo "$IP_ADDR" | { read octet1 octet2 octet3 octet4 extra;
  [[ "$octet1" == *[[:digit:]]* ]] &&
  test "$octet1" -ge 0 && test "$octet1" -le 255 &&
  [[ "$octet2" == *[[:digit:]]* ]] &&
  test "$octet2" -ge 0 && test "$octet2" -le 255 &&
  [[ "$octet3" == *[[:digit:]]* ]] &&
  test "$octet3" -ge 0 && test "$octet3" -le 255 &&
  [[ "$octet4" == *[[:digit:]]* ]] &&
```

```
            test "$octet4" -ge 0 && test "$octet4" -le 255 &&
            test -z "$extra" 2> /dev/null; }; then
            echo "${IP_ADDR} is valid"
       else
            echo "${IP_ADDR} is NOT valid"
       fi
```

8. Try running the following commands:

```
$ bash validate_ip.sh "a.a.a.a"
$ bash validate_ip.sh "0.a.a.a"
$ bash validate_ip.sh "255.255.255.255"
$ bash validate_ip.sh "0.0.0.0"
$ bash validate_ip.sh "192.168.0.10"
```

How it works...

Let's understand our script in detail:

1. First, we begin by creating the `bad_input.sh` script—it takes `$1` (or argument 1) and runs the list or `ls` command.

2. Running the following commands, we can either list everything in the directory, subdirectory, or even traverse directories backwards! This is clearly not good and security vulnerabilities have even allowed malicious hackers to traverse through a web server—the idea is to contain the input for predictable results and to control input instead of allowing everything:

```
$ touch TEST.txt
$ mkdir new_dir/
$ bash bad_input.sh "."
...
$ bash bad_input.sh "../"
../all the files backwards
```

3. In the second script, `better_input.sh`, the input is sanitized by the following steps. Additionally, one could also check whether the file being listed is in fact there as well:

    1. Remove any underscores (necessary).
    2. Remove any sets of double spaces.
    3. Replace spaces with underscores.
    4. Remove any non-alphanumeric values or anything else that is not an underscore.
    5. Then, run the `ls` command.

4. Next, running `better_input.sh` will allow us to view the current working directory or any file contained within it. Wildcards have been removed and now we cannot traverse directories.

5. To validate the form of an email, we use the `grep` command combined with a regex. We are merely looking for the form of an email account name, an @ symbol, and a domain name in the form of acme.x. It is important to note that we are not looking to see whether an email is truly valid or can make its way to the intended destination, but merely whether it fits what an email should look like. Additional tests such as testing the domain's MX or DNS mail records could extend this functionality to improve the likelihood of a user entering a valid email.

6. In the next step, we test two domain names—one without the @ symbol (invalid) and one with the @ symbol (valid). Feel free to try several combinations.

7. Validating an IP address is always something that could be done with a regex, but for the purpose of easy-to-use tools that get the job done, **read** and simple tests using **test** (and evaluations) will work just fine. In its basic form, an IP address consists of four octets (or in layman terms, four values separated by a period). Without exploring what a truly valid IP address is, normally a valid octet is between 0 and 255 (never more and never less). IP addresses can have various categories and classes called **subnets**.

8. In our examples, we know that an IP address containing alphabetic characters is not a valid IP address (excluding the periods), and that the values range between 0 and 255 per octet. `192.168.0.x` (or `192.168.1.x`) is an IP subnet many people see on their home routers.

Making a simple multi-level user menu using select

Earlier in this book, we saw that you can make a script that uses recursive functions and conditional logic to create a simple menu. It worked, but another tool that can be used is `select`. Select works using a provided list (for example, it can be a wildcard selection for files) and will give you a list, such as:

```
Select a file from the list:
1.) myfirst.file
2.) mysecond.file
You chose: mysecond.file
```

Clearly, a menu such as about is very trivial; it can be useful for utility functions and for repeatable subtasks like deleting users or modifying files/archives.

Simple select scripts could also be useful for a number of activities such as mounting a drop box, decrypting or mounting a drive, or generating administrative reports.

Getting ready

Select is already a part of the Bash shell, but it has a few less than obvious points. Select relies on three variables:

- PS3: The prompt that's echoed to the user before the menu is created
- REPLY: The index of the item selected from the array
- opt: The value of the item selected from the array—not the index

Technically, opt is not mandatory, but it is the value of the element being iterated by Select in our example. You could use another name and call it **element**, for example.

How to do it...

Let's start our activity as follows:

1. Open a terminal and create a script called select_menu.sh with the following contents:

```
#!/bin/bash
TITLE="Select file menu"
PROMPT="Pick a task:"
OPTIONS=("list" "delete" "modify" "create")

function list_files() {
  PS3="Choose a file from the list or type \"back\" to go back to
the main: "
  select OPT in *; do
    if [[ $REPLY -le ${#OPT[@]} ]]; then
      if [[ "$REPLY" == "back" ]]; then
        return
      fi
      echo "$OPT was selected"
    else
```

```
        list_files
     fi
  done
}

function main_menu() {
  echo "${TITLE}"
  PS3="${PROMPT} "
  select OPT in "${OPTIONS[@]}" "quit"; do
    case "$REPLY" in
      1 )
        # List
        list_files
        main_menu # Recursive call to regenerate the menu
      ;;
      2 )
        echo "not used"
      ;;
      3 )
        echo "not used"
      ;;
      4 )
        echo "not used"
      ;;
      $(( ${#OPTIONS[@]}+1 )) ) echo "Exiting!"; break;;
      *) echo "Invalid option. Try another one.";continue;;
    esac
  done
}

main_menu # Enter recursive loop
```

2. Execute the script using the following command:

```
$ bash select_menu.sh
```

3. Press *1* to enter the file list functionality. Enter the number of any files in the menu. Once satisfied, type "back" and press *Enter* to return to the main menu.

How it works...

Let's understand our script in detail:

1. Creating the `select_menu.sh` script was trivial, but besides the use of select, some of the concepts should look familiar: functions, return, case statements, and recursion.

2. The script enters the menu by calling the `main_menu` function and then proceeds to use select to generate a menu from the `${OPTIONS}` array. The hard-coded variable named `PS3` will output the prompt before the menu, and `$REPLY` contains the index of the item selected.

3. Pressing *1* and pressing *Enter* will cause select to walk through the items and then execute the `list_files` function. This function creates a submenu by using select for the second time to list all of the files in the directory. Selecting any directory will return a `$OPT was selected` message, but if `back` is entered, then the script will return from this function and call `main_menu` from within itself (recursion). At this point, you may select any items in the main menu.

Generating and trapping signals for cleanup

Throughout this book, you have probably pressed *Ctrl + C* or *Ctrl + Z* without knowing what was occurring—it's just like pressing *Ctrl + Alt + Delete* in another OS, right? Well, in one regard, yes—it is a signal, but the action itself is very different in Linux. A signal at the hardware level is similar to a flag or some sort of immediate notification that says *hey - something happened here*. If the appropriate listener is set up, that signal can execute some sort of functionality.

On the other hand, software signaling is far more flexible and we can use signals as *simple* notification mechanisms that are far more flexible than their hardware siblings. In Linux, *Ctrl + C* equates to SIGINT (program interrupt), which typically exits a program. It can be stopped, and other functionality such as cleanup can be executed. *Ctrl + Z* or SIGTSTP (keyboard stop) typically tells a program to be **suspended** and pushed to the background (more about jobs in a later section), but it can also be blocked—just like SIGINT.

 SIGHUP is already a signal we are familiar with—the same as with SIGKILL. We saw them when we used `disown` or exited a shell. For more information regarding signals, see the `manual page for a great signal overview`.

Getting ready

Besides using the keyboard within a program, we can also send signals to programs using the `kill` command. The `kill` command can kill programs, but these signals can also be used for reloading configurations or sending user-defined signals. The most common signals you may use are SIGHUP (1), SIGINT (2), SIGKILL(9), SIGTERM(15), SIGSTOP(17,18,23), SIGSEGV(12), and SIGUSR1(10)/SIGUSR2(12). The latter two can be defined within your program or leveraged by other developers.

The `kill` command can be used easily as follows:

```
$ kill -s SIGUSR1 <processID>
$ kill -9 <processID>
$ kill -9 `pidof myprogram.sh`
```

 The `kill` command can refer to the signal number itself or by its name. It does require a process ID number to target. This can easily be found either by searching using `ps | grep X` or by using the preceding `final` using `pidof`.

How to do it...

Let's start our activity as follows:

1. Open a terminal and begin a new script called `mytrap.sh` with the following contents:

```bash
#!/bin/bash

function setup() {
  trap "cleanup" SIGINT SIGTERM
  echo "PID of script is $$"
}

function cleanup() {
  echo "cleaning up"
  exit 1
}

setup

# Loop forever with a noop (:)
while :
do
```

```
        sleep 1
done
```

2. Execute the script with $ `bash mtrap.sh`.
3. Press *Enter* several times and watch the behavior of the program.
4. Press *Ctrl + C*; notice anything different?

How it works...

Let's understand our script in detail:

1. The `mytrap.sh` script leverages functions and the trap call. Inside of the `setup` function, we set the function to be called by the `trap` command. Therefore, when *Ctrl + C* is called, the `cleanup` function is executed.
2. Running the script will cause the script to run forever after printing out the PID of the script.
3. Pressing regular keys such as *Enter* will not have an effect on the program.
4. Pressing *Ctrl+ C* will echo `cleanup` on the console and the script will exit using the `exit` command.

Using temporary files and lock files in your program

Another mechanism or component programs and scripts often use is called a lock file. It's usually temporary (it resides in /tmp) and is sometimes used when multiple entities rely on a single source of data or need to know that other programs exist. Sometimes, it's merely the presence of a file, a particular timestamp on a file, or another simple artifact.

There are several ways to test for the existence of a file, but one important attribute that has not been demonstrated or explored is the concept of a **hidden** file. A hidden file in Linux is not really hidden (like in Windows), but it is not usually apparently unless a particular flag or command is ran. For example, the `ls` command does not return hidden files among the results, but the `ls` command with the `-a` flag will (`-a` for all).

 Most file explorers have hidden files that aren't visible by default. In Ubuntu, *Ctrl + H* inside of the file explorer toggles this feature.

To create a hidden file, a . (period) needs to be present at the beginning of a file's name:

```
$ touch .myfirsthiddenfile.txt
```

Besides the presence of any regular file, we can also use the `mktemp` command to create lock files.

Getting ready

We briefly mentioned that temporary files can reside inside the /tmp directory. Often, /tmp is home to short lived files such as lock files or information that can be volatile (destroyed on a power event without any detriment to the system). It is also usually RAM-based, which can offer performance benefits as well, especially if used as part of an inter-process communication system (more on this later in another recipe).

However, it is important to know that other programs can access your file in /tmp, so it should be secured with the sufficient permissions. It should also be given a name that is suitably random so that a filename collision does not occur.

How to do it...

Let's start our activity as follows:

1. Open a new terminal and create a new script by the name of `mylock.sh` with the following contents:

```
#!/bin.bash

LOCKFILE="/tmp/mylock"

function setup() {
  # $$ will provide the process ID
  TMPFILE="${LOCKFILE}.$$"
  echo "$$" > "${TMPFILE}"
  # Now we use hard links for atomic file operations
  if ln "${TMPFILE}" "${LOCKFILE}" 2>&- ; then
      echo "Created tmp lock"
  else
      echo "Locked by" $(<$LOCKFILE)
      rm "${TMPFILE}"
      exit 1
  fi
  trap "rm ${TMPFILE} ${LOCKFILE}" SIGINT SIGTERM SIGKILL
```

```
}

setup

echo "Door was left unlocked"

exit 0
```

2. Execute the script with the `$ bash mylock.sh` script and review the console's output.
3. Next, we know that the script is looking for a particular lock file. What happens when we create a lock file and then re-run the script?

```
$ echo "1000" > /tmp/mylock
$ bash mylock.sh
$ rm /tmp/mylock
$ bash mylock.sh
```

How it works...

Let's understand our script in detail:

1. The `mylock.sh` script reuses a couple of concepts that we are already familiar with: traps and symbolic links. We know that if a trap is called or rather, it catches a particular signal, it can clean up a lock file (as is the case in this script). Symbolic links are used since they can survive atomic operations over network file systems. If a file is present at the `LOCKFILE` location, then a lock is present. If the `LOCKFILE` is absent, the doors are open.

2. When we run `mylock.sh`, we will get the following because no lock file exists yet—including any temporary ones:

```
$ bash mylock.sh
Created tmp lock
Door was left unlocked
```

3. Since the preceding script exited correctly, the `SIGKILL` signal was handled and the temporary lockfile was removed. In this case, we want to create our own lockfiles that bypass this mechanism. Create a lockfile with a faux PID of `1000`; running the script will return `Locked by 1000`, and upon deleting the lockfile, the regular behavior will occur once more (doors are unlocked).

Leveraging timeout when waiting for command completion

Sometimes, waiting for a command to finish execution or ignoring commands until completion might not be considered a solid practice in scripting, though it does have applications:

- Where commands take variable lengths of time to complete (for example, pinging a network host)
- Where tasks or commands can be executed in such a way that the *master* script waits for the success or failure of several multiple operations

However, the important thing to note is that timeout/wait requires a process, or even a subshell so that it can be monitored (by the Process ID or PID). In this recipe, we will demonstrate the use of waiting for a subshell with the timeout command (which was added into the coreutils package 7.0) and how to do so using trap and kill (for alarms/timers).

Getting ready

In earlier recipes, we introduced the use of `trap` to catch signals, and the use of `kill` to send signals to processes. These will be explained further in this recipe, but here are three new native Bash variables:

- `$$`: Which returns the PID of the current script
- `$?`: Which returns the PID of the last job that was sent to the background
- `$@` :Which returns the array of input variables (for example, `$!`, `$2`)

 We are skirting around the ideas of jobs, tasks, background, and foreground as they will appear again in proper detail in a later administrative recipe.

How to do it...

We begin this recipe knowing that there is a command called `timeout` available to the Bash shell. However, it falls short of being able to provide the functionality of timeouts in functions within a script itself. Using `trap`, `kill`, and signals, we can set timers or `alarms` (`ALRM`) to perform clean exits from runaway functions or commands. Let's begin:

1. Open a new terminal and create a new script by the name of `mytimeout.sh` with the following contents:

```bash
#!/bin/bash

SUBPID=0

function func_timer() {
  trap "clean_up" SIGALRM
  sleep $1& wait
  kill -s SIGALRM $$
}

function clean_up() {
  trap - ALRM
  kill -s SIGALRM $SUBPID
  kill $! 2>/dev/null
}

# Call function for timer & notice we record the job's PID
func_timer $1& SUBPID=$!

# Shift the parameters to ignore $0 and $1
shift

# Setup the trap for signals SIGALRM and SIGINT
trap "clean_up" ALRM INT

# Execute the command passed and then wait for a signal
"$@" & wait $!

# kill the running subpid and wait before exit
kill -ALRM $SUBPID
wait $SUBPID
exit 0
```

2. Using a command with variable times (ping), we can test `mytimeout.sh` using the first parameter to `mytimeout.sh` as the timeout variable!

```
$ bash mytimeout.sh 1 ping -c 10 google.ca
$ bash mytimeout.sh 10 ping -c 10 google.ca
```

How it works...

You might be asking yourself, *can I put functions to the background?* Absolutely—and you could even use a command called `export` with the -f flag (although it may not be supported in all environments). If you were to use the timeout command instead, you would have to either run ONLY the command you wish to monitor or put the function inside of a second script to be called by timeout. Clearly, this is less than optimal in some situations. In this recipe, we use signals or rather, the `alarm` signal, to act as a timer. When we set the alarm with a specific variable, it will raise SIGALARM once the timer expires! If the process is still alive, we merely kill it and exit the script if we haven't already exited:

1. In step 1, we create the `mytimeout.sh` script. It uses a few of our new primitives such as `$!` to monitor the PID of the function we sent to execute in the background as a job (or subshell, in this case). We `arm` the timer and then carry on with the execution of the script. Then, we use shift to literally *shift* the parameters passed to our script to ignore `$1` (or the timeout variable). Finally, we watch for SIGALRM and perform a cleanup if necessary.

2. In step 2, `mytimeout.sh` is executed twice using the `ping` command, which is targeting `google.ca`. In the first instance, we use a timeout of 1 second, and in the second instance, we use a timeout of 10 seconds. Ping, in both cases, will perform 10 pings (for example, one ping there and back to whatever host is answering ICMP requests for the DNS entry for google.ca). The first instance will execute early, and the second allows 10 pings to execute cleanly and exit:

```
$ bash mytimeout.sh 1 ping -c 10 google.ca
PING google.ca (172.217.13.99) 56(84) bytes of data.
64 bytes from yul02s04-in-f3.1e100.net (172.217.13.99): icmp_seq=1
ttl=57 time=10.0 ms

$ bash mytimeout.sh 10 ping -c 10 google.ca
PING google.ca (172.217.13.99) 56(84) bytes of data.
64 bytes from yul02s04-in-f3.1e100.net (172.217.13.99): icmp_seq=1
ttl=57 time=11.8 ms
64 bytes from yul02s04-in-f3.1e100.net (172.217.13.99): icmp_seq=2
ttl=57 time=14.5 ms
64 bytes from yul02s04-in-f3.1e100.net (172.217.13.99): icmp_seq=3
```

```
ttl=57 time=10.8 ms
64 bytes from yul02s04-in-f3.1e100.net (172.217.13.99): icmp_seq=4
ttl=57 time=13.1 ms
64 bytes from yul02s04-in-f3.1e100.net (172.217.13.99): icmp_seq=5
ttl=57 time=12.7 ms
64 bytes from yul02s04-in-f3.1e100.net (172.217.13.99): icmp_seq=6
ttl=57 time=13.4 ms
64 bytes from yul02s04-in-f3.1e100.net (172.217.13.99): icmp_seq=7
ttl=57 time=9.15 ms
64 bytes from yul02s04-in-f3.1e100.net (172.217.13.99): icmp_seq=8
ttl=57 time=14.0 ms
64 bytes from yul02s04-in-f3.1e100.net (172.217.13.99): icmp_seq=9
ttl=57 time=12.0 ms
64 bytes from yul02s04-in-f3.1e100.net (172.217.13.99): icmp_seq=10
ttl=57 time=11.2 ms

--- google.ca ping statistics ---
10 packets transmitted, 10 received, 0% packet loss, time 9015ms
rtt min/avg/max/mdev = 9.155/12.307/14.520/1.545 ms
```

 Notice that google.ca could be replaced with another DNS name, but the times may vary depending on your location. Therefore, 10 PINGs may not actually have time to be executed fully.

Creating a file-in-file-out program and running processes in parallel

In this recipe, we use a concept called file-in-file-out (FIFO), also known as **pipes**, to pass along a parameter to several "worker" scripts. These workers operate in parallel (in other words, mostly independent of the master process), read an input, and execute a command. FIFOS are useful because they can reduce file system activities or input/output (IO), and data can flow directly to listeners or recipients. They are represented on the file system as files and are bidirectional—they can be read and written to at the same time.

Getting ready

To create FIFOs, we use the `mkinfo` command to create what appears to be a file (everything is a file in Linux). This file has a special property, though, which is different than normal files and also different from the pipes we had been previously using: the pipes, in this case, can allow for multiple readers and writers!

As with any file, you can also provide permissions using the –m flag such as this: –m a=rw, or use the `mknod` command (this isn't covered as it requires that you use a second command called `chown` to change `permissions` after creation).

How to do it...

To start this exercise, we will introduce two terms: leader and follower, or master and worker. In this case, the master (the central host) will create the workers (or minions). While the recipe is a bit contrived, it should make for an easy go-to template for a simple **named pipes** or FIFO pattern. Essentially, there is a master that creates five workers, and those newly created workers echo out what is provided to them through the named pipe:

1. To get started, open a new terminal and create two new scripts: `master.sh` and `worker.sh`.

2. In `master.sh`, add the following contents:

```bash
#!/bin/bash

FIFO_FILE=/tmp/WORK_QUEUE_FIFO
mkfifo "${FIFO_FILE}"

NUM_WORKERS=5
I=0
while [ $I -lt $NUM_WORKERS ]; do

  bash worker.sh "$I" &
  I=$((I+1))

done

I=0
while [ $I -lt $NUM_WORKERS ]; do

  echo "$I" > "${FIFO_FILE}"
  I=$((I+1))
```

```
done

sleep 5
rm -rf "${FIFO_FILE}"
exit 0
```

3. In `worker.sh`, add the following contents:

```bash
#!/bin/bash

FIFO_FILE=/tmp/WORK_QUEUE_FIFO

BUFFER=""
echo "WORKER started: $1"

while :
do

read BUFFER < "${FIFO_FILE}"

if [ "${BUFFER}" != "" ]; then
  echo "Worker received: $BUFFER"
  exit 1
fi

done

exit 0
```

4. In the terminal, run the following command and observe the output:

```
$ bash master.sh
```

How it works...

The idea of this recipe is that if you have several repetitive tasks such as bulk operations and potentially multiple cores, you can perform tasks in parallel (often seen in the Linux world as Jobs). This recipe creates a single master that spawns several worker scripts into the background, which await input from the named pipe. Once they read input from the named pipe, they will echo it to the screen and then exit. Eventually, the master will exit too, removing the pipe along with it:

1. In step 1, we open a new terminal and create the two scripts: `master.sh` and `worker.sh`.

2. In step 2, we create the `master.sh` script. It uses two while loops to create *n* numbers of worker scripts with `$I` identifiers and then sends the same number of values to the FIFO before sleeping/exit.

3. In step 3, we create the `worker.sh` script, which echos an initialization message and then waits until `$BUFFER` is not empty (NULL, as it can be sometimes referred to). Once `$BUFFER` is full or rather, contains a message, then it echos it to the console and the script exits.

4. In step 4, the console should contain an output similar to the following:

```
$ bash master.sh
WORKER started: 0
WORKER started: 1
We got 0
We got 1
WORKER started: 4
We got 2
WORKER started: 2
We got 3
WORKER started: 3
We got 4
```

With the two scripts working in tandem over the FIFO, a numeric value is passed between them and the workers perform their *work*. These values or messages could easily be modified so that the workers execute commands instead!

 Notice that the output can be in a different order. This is because Linux is not deterministic and spawning processes or reading from the FIFO might be blocked, or someone might get there before it (due to scheduling). Keep this in mind as the FIFO is also not atomic or synchronous—if you wish to designate which message goes to what host, you could create an identifier or messaging scheme.

Executing your script on startup

This recipe is not limited to running only applications or services at startup, but to also start scripts on bootup (power on) of a system. For example, if your system boots up and you would like to apply several tweaks to the OS such as performance enhancements or battery tweaks, you can do this on startup via the `systemd` or `init.d` script. Another example could be to run a never ending script that creates logging events, like an electronic version of a pulse monitor.

In short, Linux or most *NIX systems use either the venerable rc.d system or the newer and more controversial systemd system to manage the starting and stopping of system resources. Without diving into the entire boot sequence of Linux, here is how it works:

1. The Linux kernel is loaded and mounts the root filesystem.
2. The rootfile system contains a shell at a particular path (the init level).
3. Then, the systemd works its way through a series of services to start (the run level).

If a service or script is added, it will likely be added at the **run level**. It can also be started, stopped, reloaded, and restarted from the command line at any time as well. When the system is booting, it merely uses the start functionality provided by the init.d or system.d script. However, even though the semantics of either the rc.d or systemd system differ, they still require the following:

- Scripts or services need to be enabled for specific system startup levels.
- Scripts to be started and/or stopped can be configured to be started in a specific order.
- Directives for starting (at a minimum), stopping, restarting and/or reloading are executed based on a parameter when executing one of these actions (or blocks). Any number of commands can also be executed when calling start, for example.

 You may notice when scouring the web when looking for resources that a number of init systems exist: upstart, SysVinit, rc.d, procd, and the list goes on. You can refer to your distribution documentation for a current explanation on the startup system in use.

Getting ready

In Ubuntu 16.04 LTS (and other distributions), use systemd. Knowledge of both the init.d and systemd service control systems is certainly worth having as many embedded systems use Busybox. BusyBox uses the init.d system instead of systemd.

Before diving into the "how to do it" section, we are going to create a template init script for posterity and awareness should you run into them. It will be called myscript and it will run myscript.sh. At a minimum, a system.d compatible script looks like the following:

```
#!/bin/sh
### BEGIN INIT INFO
# Provides: myscript
# Required-Start: $local_fs
```

```
# Required-Stop: $local_fs
# Default-Start: 2 3 4 5
# Default-Stop: 0 1 6
# Short-Description: Start script or daemons example
### END INIT INFO

PATH=/sbin:/bin:/usr/sbin:/usr/bin
DAEMON_NAME=myscript.sh
DESC=myscript

DAEMON=/usr/sbin/$DAEMON_NAME

case $1 in
  start)
  log_daemon_msg "Starting $DESC"
  $DAEMON_NAME
  log_end_msg 0
  ;;
  stop)
  log_daemon_msg "Stopping $DESC"
  killall $DAEMON_NAME
  log_end_msg 0
  ;;
  restart|force-reload)
  $0 stop
  sleep 1
  $0 start
  ;;
  status)
  status_of_proc "$DAEMON" "$DESC" && exit 0 || exit $?
  ;;
  *)
  N=/etc/init.d/$DESC
  echo "Usage: $N {start|stop|restart|force-reload|status}" >&2
  exit 1
  ;;
esac

exit 0

# vim:noet
```

The content should be fairly easy to read if you have worked through the cookbook until this point. It relies on the comments in the header to determine the name, run levels, orders, and dependencies. Below that, it uses a switch statement while looking for several predetermined/standardized parameters: start, stop, restart, force-reload, and status. Inside of the start case, we start the binary, and in the stop case, we use the `killall` function to stop the binary.

It is important to know that the mere installation of an init script does not guarantee execution on startup. There is a process to **enable** the service or script. In the older system (SysV), you may have heard/seen of the command `chkconfig` being used. In systemd, you may use the `systemctl` command to enable/disable a service. In this section, we are only going to focus on systemd.

 SysV executes the scripts in sequential order based on their number in the filename (for example, `S99-myinit`). Systemd does not because it also reviews dependencies and waits for their completion.

How to do it...

Let's start our activity as follows:

1. Create a script called `myscript.sh` with the following contents:

```bash
#!/bin/bash

for (( ; ; ))
do
    sleep 1
done
```

2. Next, let's add the correct permissions to the script so that we can create a systemd service using it. Notice the use of the `sudo` command—enter your password where appropriate:

```
$ sudo cp myscript.sh /usr/bin
$ sudo chmod a+x /usr/bin/myscript.sh
```

3. Now that we have something to execute on start, we need to create a service configuration file to describe our service; we used `vi` in this example and `sudo` (note down its location):

```
$ sudo vi /etc/systemd/system/myscript.service
[Unit]
Description=myscript

[Service]
ExecStart=/usr/bin/myscript.sh
ExecStop=killall myscript.sh

[Install]
WantedBy=multi-user.target
```

4. To enable the `myscript` service, run the following command:

```
$ sudo systemctl enable myscript # disable instead of enable will
disable the service
```

5. To start and verify the presence of the process, run the following command:

```
$ sudo systemctl start myscript
$ sudo systemctl status myscript
```

6. You may reboot the system to see our service in action on startup.

How it works...

Let's understand our script in detail:

1. In step 1, we create a trivial looping program to be ran at system startup called `myscript.sh`.
2. In step 2, we copy the script to the `/usr/bin` directory and add permissions using the `chmod` command for everyone to be able to execute the script (`chmod a+x myscript.sh`). Notice the use of `sudo` permissions to create a file in this directory and to apply permissions.
3. In the third step, we create the service configuration file, which describes a service unit for systemd. It goes by the name of `myscript` and within the `[Service]` directive, the two most important parameters are present: `ExecStart` and `ExecStop`. Notice that the start and stop sections look similar to the SysV/init.d approach.

4. Next, we use the `systemctl` command to enable `myscript`. Conversely, it can be used in the following way to disable `myscript`: `$systemctl disable myscript`.

5. Then, we use `systemctl` to start `myscript` and verify the status of our script. You should get a similar output to the following (notice that we double checked the presence using `ps`):

```
$ sudo systemctl status myscript
myscript.service - myscript
    Loaded: loaded (/etc/systemd/system/myscript.service; enabled;
vendor preset:
    Active: active (running) since Tue 2017-12-26 14:28:51 EST; 6min
ago
 Main PID: 17966 (myscript.sh)
    CGroup: /system.slice/myscript.service
            ├─17966 /bin/bash /usr/bin/myscript.sh
            └─18600 sleep 1

Dec 26 14:28:51 moon systemd[1]: Started myscript.
$ ps aux | grep myscript
root 17966 0.0 0.0 20992 3324 ? Ss 14:28 0:00 /bin/bash
/usr/bin/myscript.sh
rbrash 18608 0.0 0.0 14228 1016 pts/20 S+ 14:35 0:00 grep --
color=auto myscript
```

6. On reboot, if enable was set, our script will be running as expected.

5
Scripts for System Administration Tasks

In this chapter, we will introduce the following topics:

- Gathering and aggregating system information
- Gathering network information and connectivity diagnostics
- Configuring basic network connectivity
- Monitoring directories and files
- Compressing and archiving files
- Rotating files from RAM to storage for log rotation
- Using Linux iptables for a firewall
- Accessing SQL databases remotely or locally
- Creating SSH keys for password less remote access
- Creating and configuring cron jobs for task scheduling
- Creating users and groups systematically

Introduction

This chapter is about performing system administration tasks common to nearly all users and we'll be looking at logs, archiving them, job/task management, network connectivity, securing systems using a firewall (IPtables), monitoring directories for changes, and creating users. We will also acknowledge that users and administrators often have to access resources from other systems for resources such as SQL or they have to use SSH to log in to another system using only cryptographic keys—no passwords required!

This chapter also serves as a crash course on some critical components in today's computing environment: **networking**. Users might not know what a port is, an IP address, or how to find **network interfaces** (**NICs**) on their computer. By the end of this chapter, beginners should be able to configure a network, and will have an improved level of competency when working with a network terminology.

Gathering and aggregating system information

In this section, we are going to discuss the `dmidecode` Linux tool, which will gather information about the system such as CPU information, server, memory, and networking.

Getting ready

Besides having a terminal open, we need to remember a few concepts:

- We are going to use some commands that will give us information about the Kernel, Linux distribution, physical server information, system uptime, network information, memory information, and CPU information.
- By using this, anyone can create scripts to gather system information.

How to do it...

1. We can get details about the Linux distribution that you are working on. These distributions have a release file that you can locate in the `/etc/` folder. Now, open a terminal and enter the following command to get the information regarding the Linux distribution you are working on:

```
cat /etc/*-release
```

2. The preceding option has an alternative, and the alternative is the version file that's present in the `/proc` folder. So, run the following command:

```
cat /proc/version
```

3. Now, run the following command to get the Kernel's information:

```
uname -a
```

4. System `uptime`: for information about this, create a script called `server_uptime.sh`:

```
server_uptime=`uptime | awk '{print $3,$4}'| sed 's/,//'| grep
"day"`;
if [[ -z "$server_uptime" ]]; then
        server_uptime=`uptime | awk '{print $3}'| sed 's/,//'`
        echo $server_uptime
else
        :;
fi;
```

5. Now, we will run the following commands to get the physical server's information:

```
$ sudo dmidecode -s system-manufacture
$ sudo dmidecode -s system-product-name
$ sudo dmidecode -s system-serial-number
```

6. Then, we will run the following command to get the CPU's information:

```
sudo dmidecode -t4|awk '/Handle / {print $2}' |sed 's/,//'
```

You can get each CPU's information from the `cpuinfo` file, which is present in the `/proc` directory.

7. Network information: We are going to get the IP address by running the following command:

```
ip a
```

To get the MAC address, run the following command:

```
ip addr show ens33
```

You may replace `ens33` with `eth0`, depending on your network interface's information.

8. Memory information: To get the total number of slots, run the following command:

```
sudo dmidecode -t17 |awk '/Handle / {print $2}'|wc -l
```

To get the total populated slots, run the following command:

```
sudo dmidecode -t17 |awk '/Size:/'|awk '!/No/'|wc -l
```

To get the total unpopulated slots, run the following command:

```
sudo dmidecode -t17 |awk '/Size:/'|awk '/No/'|wc -l
```

How it works...

After running the `cat /etc/*-release` command, press *Enter* and you will get the output according to your Linux distribution. In my case, the output is as follows:

```
DISTRIB_ID=Ubuntu
DISTRIB_RELEASE=16.04
DISTRIB_CODENAME=xenial
DISTRIB_DESCRIPTION="Ubuntu 16.04.4 LTS"
NAME="Ubuntu"
VERSION="16.04.4 LTS (Xenial Xerus)"
ID=ubuntu
ID_LIKE=Debian
PRETTY_NAME="Ubuntu 16.04.4 LTS"
VERSION_ID="16.04"
HOME_URL="http://www.ubuntu.com/"
SUPPORT_URL="http://help.ubuntu.com/"
BUG_REPORT_URL="http://bugs.launchpad.net/ubuntu/"
VERSION_CODENAME=xenial
UBUNTU_CODENAME=xenial
```

There is an alternate way to get system information. You can get the system information by running a version file from the `/proc` directory. After running the command, press *Enter*, and you will get the output according to your Linux distribution. In my case, the output is as follows:

```
Linux version 4.13.0-45-generic (buildd@lgw01-amd64-011) (gcc version 5.4.0
20160609 (Ubuntu 5.4.0-6ubuntu1~16.04.9)) #50~16.04.1-Ubuntu SMP Wed May 30
11:18:27 UTC 2018
```

`uname` is the tool that we are using to gather this information. Press *Enter* after running the command and you will get the Kernel information. In my case, the output is as follows:

```
Linux ubuntu 4.13.0-45-generic #50~16.04.1-Ubuntu SMP Wed May 30 11:18:27
UTC 2018 x86_64 x86_64 x86_64 GNU/Linux
```

Execute the $ `bash server_uptime.sh` script—press *Enter* at the prompt and you will get the uptime of the server.

To get the physical server information, we used the `dmidecode` tool. The first command is used to get the manufacturer's information, the second command is to get the model name, and the third command gets the serial number. While running a `dmidecode` command, you must be the root user.

The output snippet will look as follows:

```
0x0004
0x0005
0x0006
0x0007
```

To get each CPU's information, we created a script. Execute the $ `sudo bash cpu_info.sh` script—press *Enter* at the prompt and you will get information for each CPU.

The output snippet will look like the following:

```
CPU#000
Unknown
GenuineIntel
1800MHz
3.3V
1
CPU#001
Unknown
GenuineIntel
1800MHz
3.3V
1
CPU#002
Unknown
GenuineIntel
1800MHz
3.3V
1
CPU#003
Unknown
GenuineIntel
```

```
1800MHz
3.3V
1
```

Network information: We ran the `ip` command to get the IP address and MAC address.

Memory information: We used the `dmidecode` tool to get the memory information such as the total number of slots, and the total populated and unpopulated slots. You must be the root user to run this command.

Gathering network information and connectivity diagnostics

In this section, we are going to test IPv4's connectivity and write scripts for it.

Getting ready

Besides having a terminal open, we need to remember a few concepts:

- The If..Else condition case in shell scripting
- IP address of the device
- `curl` command must be installed (you can install it by using the following command: `sudo apt install curl`)

The purpose of this section is to show you how you can check network connectivity.

How to do it...

1. Open a terminal and create the `test_ipv4.sh` script:

```
if ping -q -c 1 -W 1 8.8.8.8 >/dev/null; then
  echo "IPv4 is up"
else
  echo "IPv4 is down"
fi
```

2. Now, to test IP connectivity and DNS, create a script called `test_ip_dns.sh`:

```
if ping -q -c 1 -W 1 google.com >/dev/null
then
  echo "The network is up"
else
  echo "The network is down"
fi
```

3. Lastly, create a script called `test_web.sh` to test web connectivity:

```
case "$(curl -s --max-time 2 -I http://google.com | sed 's/^[^ ]*
*\([0-9]\).*/\1/; 1q')" in
  [23]) echo "HTTP connectivity is up";;
  5) echo "The web proxy won't let us through";;
  *) echo "The network is down or very slow";;
esac
```

How it works...

1. Execute the script as `$ bash test_ipv4.sh`. Here, we are checking the connection with the `8.8.8.8` IP address. For that, we use the `ping` command in the `if` condition. If the condition is `true`, we will get the statement written and printed on the screen as an if block. If not, the statement in `else` will be printed.

2. Execute the script as `$ bash test_ip_dns.sh`. Here, we are testing the connectivity using the hostname. We are also passing the `ping` command in the `if` condition and checking if the network is up or not. If the condition is `true`, we will get the statement written in an `if` block that's printed on the screen. If not, the statement in `else` will be printed.

3. Execute the script as `$ bash test_web.sh`. Here, we are testing the web connectivity. We use the `case` statement here. We are using the curl tool in this case, which is used to transfer data to and from a server.

Configuring basic network connectivity

In this section, we are going to configure basic network connectivity using `wpa_supplicant`.

Getting ready

Besides having a terminal open, we need to remember a few concepts:

- Check whether `wpa_supplicant` is installed or not.
- You should know the SSID and password.
- Remember that you have to run your program as a root user.

How to do it...

Create a script called `wifi_conn.sh` and write the following code in it:

```bash
#!/bin/bash
ifdown wlan0
rm /etc/network/interfaces
touch /etc/network/interfaces
echo 'auto lo' >> /etc/network/interfaces
echo 'iface lo inet loopback' >> /etc/network/interfaces
echo 'iface eth0 inet dhcp' >> /etc/network/interfaces
echo 'allow-hotplug wlan0' >> /etc/network/interfaces
echo 'iface wlan0 inet manual' >> /etc/network/interfaces
echo 'wpa-roam /etc/wpa_supplicant/wpa_supplicant.conf' >> /etc/network/interfaces
echo 'iface default inet dhcp' >> /etc/network/interfaces
rm /etc/wpa_supplicant/wpa_supplicant.conf
touch /etc/wpa_supplicant/wpa_supplicant.conf
echo 'ctrl_interface=DIR=/var/run/wpa_supplicant GROUP=netdev' >> /etc/wpa_supplicant/wpa_supplicant.conf
echo 'update_config=1' >> /etc/wpa_supplicant/wpa_supplicant.conf
wpa_passphrase $1 $2 >> /etc/wpa_supplicant/wpa_supplicant.conf
ifup wlan0
```

How it works...

Execute the script using `sudo`:

```
sudo bash wifi_conn.sh <SSID> <password>
```

Monitoring directories and files

inotify is a tool in Linux which is used to report when a file system event occurs. Using inotify, you can monitor individual files or directories.

Getting ready

Make sure you have the inotify tool installed on your system.

How to do it...

Create a script called inotify_example.sh:

```
#! /bin/bash
folder=~/Desktop/abc
cdate=$(date +"%Y-%m-%d-%H:%M")
inotifywait -m -q -e create -r --format '%:e %w%f' $folder | while read
file
do
    mv ~/Desktop/abc/output.txt ~/Desktop/Old_abc/${cdate}-output.txt
done
```

How it works...

The inotifywait command is mostly used in shell scripting. The main purpose of the inotify tool is to monitor the directories and new files. It also monitors the changes in the files.

Compressing and archiving files

There is a difference between a compressed and an archive file. So, what is an archive file? It is a collection of files and directories that are stored in a single file. An archive file is not a compressed file.

What is a compressed file? This is a collection of files and directories stored in one file. It uses less disk space for storage.

In this section, we are going to discuss two compression tools:

- `bzip2`
- `zip`

Getting ready

You should have files to archive and compress.

How to do it...

First, let's see how we can compress the files:

1. We are going to look at compression with the help of `bzip2`. Decide which file to compress and run the following command:

   $ bzip2 *filename*

   Using `bzip2`, we can compress multiple files and directories at the same time. Just separate them by putting a space between each of them. You can compress it as follows:

   $ bzip2 file1 file2 file3 /student/work

2. We are going to use `zip` for compression. By using the zip compression tool, files are compressed individually:

   $ zip -r file_name.zip files_dir

After running the preceding command, the file to be compressed or the directory to be compressed, such as `files_zip` will be compressed and you will get a compressed file called `file_name.zip`. The `-r` option includes all the files in the `files_dir` directory recursively.

Now, let's discuss how to archive files:

An archive file contains more than one file or directory. **Tar** is used to archive files without compression.

The following are the two archiving modes:

- −x: extract an archive
- −c: create an archive

Options:

- −f: FILE name of the archive—you must specify this unless using tape drive for archive
- −v: Be verbose, list all files being archived/extracted
- −z: Create/extract archive with gzip/gunzip
- −j: Create/extract archive with bzip2/bunzip2
- −J: Create/extract archive with XZ

To create a TAR file, use the following command:

```
$ tar -cvf filename.tar directory/file
```

In this example, we are representing a file, which is created when we use the `tar` command. Its name is `filename.tar`. We can specify the directory or file in which we are putting archive files. We must specify it after inserting `filename.tar`. Multiple files and directories can archive at the same time, just leave a space between the file and directory names:

```
$ tar -cvf filename.tar /home/student/work /home/student/school
```

After executing the preceding command, all the contents from work and school directories will be stored in the new file `filename.tar`.

After running the preceding command, all the contents from work and school subdirectories will be stored in the new file `filename.tar`.

The following command is used to list the contents of a TAR file:

```
$ tar -tvf filename.tar
```

To extract the contents of a TAR file, use the following command:

```
$ tar -xvf filename.tar
```

This command is used for extraction and it will not remove the TAR file. However, in your current working directory, you will find the unarchived contents.

How it works...

bzip2 is used to compress the files and folder at the same time. Just issue the command in the terminal and the files will be compressed. After the compression, the compressed file will get the extension `.bz2`.

zip compress the files individually and then collects them in a single file.

A TAR file is a collection of different files and directories, which combines them into one file. TAR is used for creating backups and archives.

Rotating files from RAM to storage for log rotation

In this section, we are going to discuss the logrotate Linux tool. Using this tool, administration of systems becomes easy. The systems generate large number of log files. This allows for automatic rotation, removal, compression, and mailing of log files.

We can handle each and every log file. We can handle them daily, weekly, and monthly. Using this tool, we can keep logs longer with less disk space. The default configuration file is `/etc/logrotate.conf`. Run the following command to see the contents of this file:

```
$ cat /etc/logrotate.conf
```

You will see the following:

```
weekly
rotate 4
create

include /etc/logrotate.d
# no packages own wtmp, or btmp -- we'll rotate them here
/var/log/wtmp {
    missingok
    monthly
    create 0664 root utmp
    rotate 1
}

/var/log/btmp {
    missingok
    monthly
    create 0660 root utmp
```

```
    rotate 1
}

# system-specific logs may be configured here
```

Getting ready

To use logrotator, you must be aware of the `logrotate` command.

How to do it...

We are going to look at an example configuration.

We have two options for managing log files:

1. Create a new configuration file and store it in `/etc/logrotate.d/`. This configuration file will be executed daily along with other standard jobs. This will be with root privileges.
2. Create a new configuration file and execute it independently. This will execute with non-root privileges. This way, you can execute it manually, at whatever times you want.

Adding configuration to /etc/logrotate.d/

Now, we will configure a web server. This puts information like `access.log` and `error.log` into the `/var/log/example-app`. It will act as a data user or group.

To add some configuration to `/etc/logrotate.d/`, first open up a new file there:

```
$ sudo nano /etc/logrotate.d/example-app
```

Write the following code in `example-app`:

```
/var/log/example-app/*.log {
    daily
    missingok
    rotate 14
    compress
    notifempty
    create 0640 www-data www-data
    sharedscripts
    postrotate
```

```
        systemctl reload example-app
    endscript
}
```

Some of the new configuration directives in this file are as follows:

- `create 0640 www-data www-data`: After rotation, this will create a new empty log file with specified permissions for the owner and group.
- `sharedscripts`: This means that configuration scripts are run only once per run instead of there being a rotation for each file.
- `postrotate` to `endscript`: This particular block has a script that has code for running after the log file is rotated. Using this, our application can switch over to the newly created log file.

How it works...

We can customize the `.config` file according to our needs and then save that file in `/etc/logrotate.d`. For that, run the following command:

```
$ sudo logrotate /etc/logrotate.conf --debug
```

After running this command, logrotate will point the standard configuration file, and then it will be on debug mode. It will give us the information about the files which logrotate is handling.

Using Linux iptables for a firewall

In this section, we are going to set up a firewall using iptables. **iptables** is the standard firewall software present in most Linux distributions. We are going to use these set of rules to filter the network traffic. You can protect the server from unwanted traffic by filtering the data packets by specifying the source or destination IP address, port addresses, protocol types, network interfaces, and so on. We can configure this for accepting, rejecting, or forwarding network packets.

Rules are arranged in chains. By default, there are three chains (input, output, and forward). The input chain handles incoming traffic, while the output chain handles outgoing traffic. The forward chain handles routing traffic. Each chain has a default policy to adhere to if network packets do not match any policy inside the chain.

Getting ready

Please check that the following requirements are satisfied before proceeding to the next activity:

- Root privileges
- SSH access (command line access to the server)
- Make sure you have gt and looptools installed in your Linux environment
- Basic skills for working on a Linux environment

How to do it...

Now, we are going to see some of the `iptables` commands:

1. Run the following command to list all the rules that are set on the server:

   ```
   $ sudo iptables -L
   ```

2. To allow incoming traffic from a specific port, use the following command:

   ```
   $ sudo iptables -A INPUT -p tcp --dport 4321 -j ACCEPT
   ```

   This rule will allow incoming traffic from port `4321`. The firewall needs to be restarted to make this rule effective.

   Using `iptables`, you can block the incoming traffic. For that, run the following command:

   ```
   $ sudo iptables -A INPUT -j DROP
   ```

3. If any new rules are added in the `iptables`, we should save them first. Otherwise, after a system reboot, they will disappear. Run the following command to saving the `iptables` after adding new rules:

   ```
   $ sudo iptables-save
   ```

4. The default file where rules are saved might differ depending on which Linux distribution you are working on.

5. We can save rules in a specific file by using the following command:

```
$ sudo iptables-save > /path/to/the/file
```

6. You can restore these rules that are saved in the file. Run the following command:

```
$ sudo iptables-restore > /path/to/the/file
```

How it works...

Using iptables, we can control the incoming traffic, drop the traffic on a specific port, and add new rules and save them.

Accessing SQL databases remotely or locally

In this section, we are going to learn how to automate SQL queries by connecting to a server using a shell script. Bash scripting is used for automating things.

Getting ready

Make sure that mysql, postgres, and sqlite are installed. Ensure that the user is created in MySQL and that you have granted permission to that user.

How to do it...

1. MySQL queries in script: We are going to write a script called mysql_version.sh to get the latest version of MySQL:

```
#!/bin/bash
mysql -u root -pTraining2@^ <<MY_QUERY
SELECT VERSION();
MY_QUERY
```

Now, we are going to create a script called `create_database.sh` to create the database:

```
#!/bin/bash
mysql -u root -pTraining2@^ <<MY_QUERY
create database testdb;
MY_QUERY
```

2. SQLite queries in script: Now, we are going to create a `sqlite` database. You can create the `sqlite` database by simply writing `sqlite3` and a name for the database. For example:

   $ sqlite3 testdb

   Now, we are going to create a table in the `sqlite` console. Enter `sqlite3 testdb` and press *Enter*—you will see the sqlite3 console. Now, write the `create table` command to create a table:

   ```
   $  sqlite3 testdb
   SQLite version 3.11.0 2016-02-15 17:29:24
   Enter ".help" for usage hints.
   sqlite> .databases
   seq  name              file
   ---  ---------------   -----------------------------------------
   --------------
   0    main              /home/student/testdb
   sqlite> CREATE TABLE bookslist(title text, author text);
   sqlite> .tables
   bookslist
   ```

3. Postgres queries in scripting: Now, we are going to check the postgresql database version. Here, `testdb` is our database name, which is what we created earlier. For that, run the following command:

   ```
   student@ubuntu:~$ sudo -i -u postgres
   postgres@ubuntu:~$ psql
   psql (9.5.13)
   Type "help" for help.
   postgres=# create database testdb;
   CREATE DATABASE
   postgres=# \quit
   postgres@ubuntu:~$ psql testdb
   psql (9.5.13)
   Type "help" for help.
   testdb=# select version();
   ```

```
                                                           version
---------------------------------------------------------------------
------------------------
 PostgreSQL 9.5.13 on x86_64-pc-linux-gnu, compiled by gcc (Ubuntu
5.4.0-6ubuntu1~16.04.9) 5.4.0 20160609, 64-bit
(1 row)
```

4. Now, we are going to create a table. For that, run the following command:

```
postgres@ubuntu:~$ psql testdb
psql (9.5.13)
Type "help" for help.
testdb=# create table employee(id integer, name text, address text,
designation text, salary integer);
CREATE TABLE
testdb=#
```

How it works...

1. We are creating bash scripts to check the version of a database and to create a new database. In these scripts, we are using the root user and there is a password present right after -p for that user. You can use the root user or else you can create a new user, assign a password to it, and use that user in your scripts.

2. SQLite software provides us with a simple command-line interface. Using this interface, we can manually enter and execute SQL commands. You can list the database using the dot (.) operator. .databases and .tables are used to list all the tables in the database.

3. In PostgreSQL, first we are changing the user from student to postgres. Then, we enter psql to start the postgres command-line console. In that console, we must create the testdb database. To come out of the console, run the \quit command. Now, once again, start the testdb console by typing psql testdb and pressing *Enter*. Now, create a table in that database.

Creating SSH keys for password less remote access

In this section, we are going to learn how to log in without a password using SSH. **SSH** is an open source network protocol and is used to log in to the remote servers to perform some actions. We can use the SSH protocol to transfer files from one computer to another. SSH uses public key cryptography.

Getting ready

Make sure you have SSH access.

How to do it...

1. First, we are going to create a SSH key. The `ssh-keygen` command is used to create a SSH key. Run the command as follows:

   ```
   $ ssh-keygen
   ```

   You will get the following output:

   ```
   Generating public/private rsa key pair.
   Enter file in which to save the key
   (/home/student/.ssh/id_rsa): /home/student/keytext
   Enter passphrase (empty for no passphrase):
   Enter same passphrase again:
   Your identification has been saved in /home/student/keytext.
   Your public key has been saved in /home/student/keytext.pub.
   The key fingerprint is:
   SHA256:6wmj6l9EcjufZhvwQ+iKIqEchOlmtEwC/x5rMyoKyeY
   student@ubuntu
   The key's randomart image is:
   +---[RSA 2048]----+
   |                 |
   |.                |
   |oo   . o         |
   |o.=  + o         |
   |.* o  * S        |
   |oo* oo * o       |
   |=*.. o= X        |
   |0. .*+ * =        |
   |+E==+o  +        |
   ```

```
+----[SHA256]-----+
```

2. Now, we will copy the SSH public key to the remote host. Run the following command:

```
$ ssh-copy-id remote_hostname
```

3. Now, you can log in to the remote host without a password. Run the `ssh` command as follows:

```
$ ssh remote_hostname
```

Creating and configuring cron Jobs for task scheduling

In this section, we are going to learn how to configure Cron Jobs. We are going to use crontab to set up a Cron Job.

How to do it...

1. Open your terminal and go to the `/etc` folder and check the `/cron` folders. You will see the following cron folders:
   - `/etc/cron.hourly`
   - `/etc/cron.daily`
   - `/etc/cron.weekly`
   - `/etc/cron.monthly`

2. Now, we will copy our shell script into one the preceding folders.
3. If you need to run your shell script to run daily, place it in the `cron.daily` folder. If you need to run it hourly, place it in the `cron.hourly` folder, and so on.
4. Example: Write a script and place it in the `cron.daily` folder. Make the script executable by giving the necessary permissions.
5. Now, run the `crontab` command:

```
$ crontab -e
```

6. Press *Enter* and it will ask for the editor of your type. By default, it will open `vi` editor. In my case, I selected `nano`. Now, create a `cron` command. The syntax for creating the `cron` command is:

    - The number of minutes after the hour (0 to 59)
    - The hour in military time (24 hour) format (0 to 23)
    - The day of the month (1 to 31)
    - The month (1 to 12)
    - The day of the week (0 or 7 is Sunday, or use the appropriate name)
    - The command to run

7. If you enter * in all options before the script name, you script will execute, every minute of every hour, of every day of the month, of every month and every day in the week.

8. Now, add the following line in your script:

    ```
    * * * * * /etc/name_of_cron_folder/script.sh
    ```

9. Save the file and exit.

10. You can list the existing jobs by running the following command:

    ```
    $ crontab -l
    ```

11. To remove the existing Cron Job, delete the line that contains your Cron Job and save it. Run the following command:

    ```
    $ crontab -e
    ```

How it works...

We used the `crontab` command to add and delete the Cron Job. Use the appropriate settings to execute your script daily, hourly, monthly, and weekly.

Creating users and groups systematically

In this section, we are going to learn how to create users and groups through a shell script.

How to do it...

Now, we will create a script to add a user. The useradd command is used to create a user. We are going to use the while loop, which will read our .csv file, and we will use the for loop to add each user that's present in that .csv file.

Create a script using add_user.sh:

```
#!/bin/bash
#set -x
MY_INPUT='/home/mansijoshi/Desktop'
declare -a SURNAME
declare -a NAME
declare -a USERNAME
declare -a DEPARTMENT
declare -a PASSWORD
while IFS=, read -r COL1 COL2 COL3 COL4 COL5 TRASH;
do
    SURNAME+=("$COL1")
    NAME+=("$COL2")
    USERNAME+=("$COL3")
    DEPARTMENT+=("$COL4")
    PASSWORD+=("$COL5")
done <"$MY_INPUT"
for index in "${!USERNAME[@]}"; do
    useradd -g "${DEPARTMENT[$index]}" -d "/home/${USERNAME[$index]}" -s
/bin/bash -p "$(echo "${PASSWORD[$index]}" | openssl passwd -1 -stdin)"
"${USERNAME[$index]}"
done
```

How it works...

In this recipe, we have used while and for loops. The while loop will read our .csv file. It will create arrays for each column. We used -d for the home directory, -s for the bash shell, and -p for the password.

6
Scripts for Power Users

In this chapter, we will cover the following:

- Creating Syslog entries and generating an alarm
- Backing up and erasing media, disks, and partitions with DD
- Creating graphics and presentations on the CLI
- Checking for file integrity and tampering
- Mounting network file systems and retrieving files
- Browsing the web from the CLI
- Capturing network traffic headlessly
- Finding binary dependencies
- Fetching time from different locations
- Encrypting/decrypting files from a script

Introduction

This chapter will help power users to get an idea on how to perform certain tasks with shell scripts. These tasks include creating syslog entries using the `logger` command, taking backups, creating graphics and presentations on the CLI, checking file integrity and tampering, mounting network file systems and retrieving files, browsing the web, capturing network traffic, finding binary dependencies, and encrypting and decrypting a files. In this chapter, users will learn how to use scripts to do these tasks.

Creating Syslog entries and generating an alarm

In this section, we are going to discuss the syslog protocol. We'll also learn about the `logger` command, which is a shell command and acts as an interface for the syslog module. The `logger` command makes entries in the system log. In this section, we are also going to create an alarm using a script.

Getting ready

Besides having a terminal open, we need to make sure you have a file to make an entry.

How to do it...

1. We are going to use the `logger` command to enter `file_name` into the `syslog` file. Run the following command:

   ```
   $ logger -f file_name
   ```

2. Now we are going to write a script to create an alarm. Create a `create_alarm.sh` script and write the following code in it:

   ```
   #!/bin/bash
   declare -i H
   declare -i M
   declare -i cur_H
   declare -i cur_M
   declare -i min_left
   declare -i hour_left
   echo -e "What time do you Wake Up?"
   read H
   echo -e "and Minutes?"
   read  M
   cur_H=`date +%H`
   cur_M=`date +%M`
   echo "You Selected "
   echo "$H:$M"
   echo -e "\nIt is Currently $cur_H:$cur_M"
   if [  $cur_H -lt $H ]; then
        hour_left=`expr $H - $cur_H`
        echo "$H - $cur_H means You Have: $hour_left hours still"
   ```

```
fi
if [ $cur_H -gt $H ]; then
    hour_left=`expr $cur_H - $H`
    echo -e   "\n$cur_H - $H means you have $hour_left hours left
\n"
fi
if [ $cur_H == $H ]; then
    hour_left=0
    echo -e "Taking a nap?\n"
fi
if [ $cur_M -lt $M ]; then
    min_left=`expr $M - $cur_M`
    echo -e "$M -$cur_M you have: $min_left minutes still"
fi
if [ $cur_M -gt $M ]; then
    min_left=`expr $cur_M - $M`
    echo -e "$cur_M - $M you have $min_left minutes left \n"
fi
if [ $cur_M == $M ]; then
    min_left=0
    echo -e "and no minutes\n"
fi

echo -e "Sleeping for $hour_left hours and $min_left minutes \n"
sleep $hour_left\h
sleep $min_left\m
mplayer ~/.alarm/alarm.mp3
```

How it works...

Now we will see a description of the logger command and the create_alarm script we just wrote:

1. The logger command made an entry about your file in the syslog file, which was in the /var/log directory of your system. You can check that file. Navigate to the /var/log directory and run nano syslog and you will find the entry in that file.

2. We created a script to create an alarm. We used the date command for the date and time. We also used the sleep command to block the alarm for that particular time.

Backing up and erasing media, disks, and partitions with DD

In this section, we are going to discuss the dd command. The dd command stands for *data duplicator*. It is mainly used for converting and copying files. In this section, we are going to learn about backing up and erasing a media file.

Getting ready

Besides having a terminal open, we need to make sure you have the necessary files present in the current directory to take backups, to make copies, and similar tasks.

How to do it...

The dd command is mainly used for converting and copying files. The if parameter stands for input-file and is a source. of stands for output-file and is a source where we want to paste data.

1. Run the following command to copy the contents of one file to another:

```
# create a file 01.txt and add some content in that file.
# create another file 02.txt and add some content in that file.
$ dd if=/home/student/work/01.txt of=/home/student/work/02.txt
bs=512 count=1
```

2. Run the following command to take a backup of the partition or the hard disk:

```
$ sudo dd if=/dev/sda2 of=/home/student/hdbackup.img
```

3. The dd command is also used to erase all of the contents of the disk. Run the following command to delete the contents:

```
$ sudo dd if=/home/student/work/1.sh
```

How it works...

Now we will see how the preceding commands work:

1. We used the dd command to copy the contents of the 01.txt file into the 02.txt file.

2. To run this command, we must have super user privileges. Using the dd command, we took a backup and stored it in the hdbackup.img file.

3. Using the dd command, we erased the contents of the 1.sh file.

Creating graphics and presentations on the CLI

In this section, we are going to learn how to make presentations and how to create graphics on the CLI. For this, we are going to use a tool named **dialog.** dialog is a Linux command-line tool used for taking input from users and to create message boxes.

Getting ready

Besides having a terminal open, make sure you have the dialog utility installed on your system. Install it by using the apt command. APT stands for Advanced Package Tool. Using the apt command, you can manage software from the command line for debian-based Linux. The apt command easily interacts with the dpkg packaging system.

How to do it...

1. We are going to write a script for a Yes/No box. In that script, we are going to use the if condition. Create the yes_no.sh script and add the following content to it:

```
dialog --yesno "Do you wish to continue?" 0 0
a=$?
if [ "${a}" == "0" ]; then
    echo Yes
else
    echo No
fi
```

2. We'll use dialog's calendar. Create a `calendar_dialog.sh` script. In that, we'll select a specific date:

```
dialog --calendar "Select a date... " 0 0 1 1 2018
val=$?
```

3. We're going to use the checklist option of `dialog`. Create a `checklist_dialog.sh` script. In that, we'll select multiple options:

```
dialog --stdout --checklist "Enable the account options you want:"
10 40 3 \
              1 "Home directory" on \
              2 "Signature file" off \
              3 "Simple password" off
```

4. Now, we are going to write a script to raise the border of an image. Create a `raise_border.sh` script. We'll use the `convert` command with the `raise` option:

```
convert -raise 5x5 mountain.png mountain-raised.png
```

How it works...

Now we will see a description of the options and commands written in the preceding scripts:

1. We wrote code for a Yes/No box using the dialog tool in Linux. We used the `if` condition to take an answer of either Yes or No.
2. We used the `--calendar` option of the dialog tool. It asks for a date to be selected. We selected a date from the year 2018.
3. We used the `checklist` option of the dialog tool. We made a checklist, which had three options: Home directory, Signature file, and Simple Password.
4. We raised the border of an image using the `convert` command and the `-raise` option, and then the new image was saved as `mountain-raised.png`.

Checking for file integrity and tampering

In this section, we are going to learn how to check the integrity of a file and how to check for tampering by writing a simple shell script. Why do we need to check integrity? The answer is simple: administrators check integrity when there are passwords and libraries present on a server, as well as when files contain highly sensitive data.

Getting ready

Besides having a terminal open, you need to make sure the necessary files and directories are present.

How to do it...

1. We are going to write a script to check whether a file in a directory has been tampered with. Create an `integrity_check.sh` script and add the following code to it:

```
#!/bin/bash
E_DIR_NOMATCH=50
E_BAD_DBFILE=51
dbfile=Filerec.md5
# storing records.
set_up_database ()
{
    echo ""$directory"" > "$dbfile"
    # Write directory name to first line of file.
    md5sum "$directory"/* >> "$dbfile"
    # Append md5 checksums and filenames.
}
check_database ()
{
    local n=0
    local filename
    local checksum
    if [ ! -r "$dbfile" ]
    then
        echo "Unable to read checksum database file!"
        exit $E_BAD_DBFILE
    fi

    while read rec[n]
    do
```

```
                          directory_checked="${rec[0]}"
                          if [ "$directory_checked" != "$directory" ]
                          then
                              echo "Directories do not match up!"
                              # Tried to use file for a different directory.
                              exit $E_DIR_NOMATCH
                          fi
                          if [ "$n" -gt 0 ]
                          then
                              filename[n]=$( echo ${rec[$n]} | awk '{ print $2 }' )
                              # md5sum writes recs backwards,
                              #+ checksum first, then filename.
                              checksum[n]=$( md5sum "${filename[n]}" )
                              if [ "${rec[n]}" = "${checksum[n]}" ]
                              then
                                  echo "${filename[n]} unchanged."
                              else
                                  echo "${filename[n]} : CHECKSUM ERROR!"
                              fi
                          fi
                  let "n+=1"
                  done <"$dbfile" # Read from checksum database file.
}
if [ -z "$1" ]
then
    directory="$PWD" # If not specified,
 else
    directory="$1"
fi
clear
if [ ! -r "$dbfile" ]
then
    echo "Setting up database file, \""$directory"/"$dbfile"\".";
    echo
    set_up_database
fi
check_database
echo
exit 0
```

How it works...

When we run this script, it will create a database file named `filerec.md5`, which will have data about all the files present in that directory. We'll use those files for reference.

Mounting network file systems and retrieving files

In this section, we are going to learn about the `mount` command. To mount a file system onto the file system tree, use the `mount` command. This command will instruct the kernel to mount the file system found on a particular device. There is a mount point in the tree for each partition that is mounted.

Getting ready

Besides having a terminal open, make sure you have necessary files and directories present to mount

How to do it...

1. We are going to use the `mount` command to mount the file system. Then, we are going to use the `ro` and `noexec` options to mount:

   ```
   $ mount -t ext4 /directorytobemounted /directoryinwhichitismounted
   -o ro,noexec
   ```

2. We can mount the device with default options too. Run the following command to mount a device using the default options:

   ```
   $ mount -t ext4 /directorytobemounted /directoryinwhichitismounted
   -o defaults
   ```

3. The `scp` command is used to securely transfer files between two hosts. We can transfer files from our localhost to a remote host, and also between two remote hosts. Run the following command to transfer files from a remote host to our local host:

```
$ scp from_host_name:filename /local_directory_name
```

How it works...

1. We used the `ext4` file system. In the `mount` command, we first specified which directory we wanted to mount, followed by the directory in which we will mount it with the `ro` and `noexec` options.
2. We mounted the directories using the default options.
3. We used the `scp` command to copy files from a remote host to the local host.

Browsing the web from the CLI

In this section, we are going learn about browsing the web from the command-line interface. We are going to browse the web from the command line using the w3m and ELinks browsers.

w3m is a text-based web browser. Using w3m, we can browse web pages through our terminal window.

ELinks is also a text-based web browser. It supports menu-driven configuration, frames, tables, browsing, and background downloading. ELinks can handle remote URLS as well as local files.

Getting ready

Besides having a terminal open, we need to remember a couple of things:

- Make sure you have w3m installed
- Make sure you have ELinks installed

How to do it...

1. We are going to use see how to use `w3m` to browse the web from the command line. After successful installation, just go to the terminal window and type `w3m` followed by the website name:

   ```
   $ w3m google.com
   ```

2. We are going to see how to use `elinks` to browse the web from the command line. After successful installation, just go to the terminal window and type `elinks` followed by the website name:

   ```
   $ elinks google.com
   ```

How it works...

1. To navigate through the website, use the following keyboard combinations:
   1. *Shift + U*: This combination will open a new web page
   2. *Shift + B*: This combination will navigate you to the previous web page
   3. *Shift + T*: This combination will open a new tab
2. The following are keyboard shortcuts to navigate through the website using ELinks:
   1. Go to URL - g
   2. Open a new tab - t
   3. Go forward - u
   4. Go back - Left
   5. Exit - q
   6. Previous tab - <
   7. Next tab - >
   8. Close tab - c

Capturing network traffic headlessly

In this section, we are going to learn how to capture traffic. We are going to capture network traffic with a packet sniffer tool called **tcpdump**. This tool is used to filter or capture TCP/IP packets that are transferred or received over a network.

Getting ready

Besides having a terminal open, we need to remember a few concepts:

- Make sure the tcpdump tool is installed on your machine

How to do it...

Now we are going to use some `tcpdump` commands to capture packets:

1. To capture packets from an interface, use the following code:

   ```
   $ sudo tcpdump -i eth0
   ```

2. To print the captured packets in ASCII values, use the following code:

   ```
   $ sudo tcpdump -A -i eth0
   ```

3. To capture a specific number of packets, use the following code:

   ```
   $ sudo tcpdump -c 10 -i eth0
   ```

4. To print the captured packets in HEX and ASCII, use the following code:

   ```
   $ sudo tcpdump -XX -i eth0
   ```

5. To capture and save the packets in a specific file, use the following code:

   ```
   $ sudo tcpdump -w 111.pcap -i eth0
   ```

6. To capture IP address packets, use the following code:

   ```
   $ sudo tcpdump -n -i eth0
   ```

7. To read the captured packets, use the following code:

   ```
   $ sudo tcpdump -r 111.pcap
   ```

Now we are going to look at an explanation of `tcpdump` and the commands we are using.

How it works...

We used the tcpdump Linux tool, which is used to capture or filter data packets. tcpdump is used to capture a packet on a specific interface. We used the −i option for this. We can save captured packets in a file. Just give the filename and specify the −w option in the tcpdump command. We can read the file by giving the −r option to read the file in the tcpdump command.

Finding binary dependencies

In this section, we are going to check the executable. We will find out which string is present in it by using the string command.

Getting ready

Besides having a terminal open, make sure you have a binary present in your directory.

How to do it...

1. First, we will check the executable. Run the following command:

   ```
   $ file binary_name
   ```

2. Now we will write a command to find strings within the binary. Run the following command:

   ```
   $ strings binary_name
   ```

3. We can hexdump a file by running the following command:

   ```
   $ od -tx1 binary_name
   ```

4. We can list the symbols in the binary by running the following command:

   ```
   $ nm binary_name
   ```

5. You can check which shared library it has been linked with by running the following command:

```
$ ldd binary_name
```

How it works...

Now we will look at an explanation of the previous commands:

1. We used the `file` command to get the information about the binary. We also got the architecture information by running the `file` command.
2. The `string` command will return the string within that binary file.
3. By running the `od` command, you will get the hexdump of the file.
4. There are symbols present in the binary. You can list those symbols by running the `nm` command.
5. By running the `ldd` command, you can check which shared library your binary is linked with.

Fetching time from different locations

In this section, we are going to learn how to use the `date` command to fetch time from different time zones.

Getting ready

Besides having a terminal open, you need to have a basic knowledge of `date` command.

How to do it...

1. We are going to write a shell script to ascertain the time in different time zones. To do this, we are going to use the `date` command. Create a `timezones.sh` shell script and write the following code in it:

```
TZ=":Antarctica/Casey" date
TZ=":Atlantic/Bermuda" date
TZ=":Asia/Calcutta" date
TZ=":Europe/Amsterdam" date
```

How it works...

In the preceding script, we used the `date` command to fetch the time. We fetched the time from four different continents—Antarctica, Atlantic, Asia, and Europe.

You can find all of the time zones in the `/usr/share/zoneinfo` folder on your system.

Encrypting/decrypting files from a script

In this section, we are going to learn about OpenSSL. In this section, we are going encrypt and decrypt messages and files using OpenSSL.

Getting ready

Besides having a terminal open, you need to have a basic knowledge of encoding and decoding schemes.

How to do it...

1. We are going to encrypt and decrypt simple messages. We will use the -base64 encoding scheme. First, we will encrypt a message. Run the following command in the terminal:

   ```
   $ echo "Welcome to Bash Cookbook" | openssl enc -base64
   ```

2. To decrypt the message, run following command in the terminal:

   ```
   $ echo " V2VsY29tZSB0byBCYXNoIENvb2tib29rCg==" | openssl enc -base64 -d
   ```

3. Now we are going to encrypt and decrypt files. First, we will encrypt a file. Run the following command in the terminal:

   ```
   $ openssl enc -aes-256-cbc -in /etc/services -out enc_services.dat
   ```

4. Now we are going to decrypt a file. Run the following command in the terminal:

   ```
   $ openssl enc -aes-256-cbc -d -in enc_services.dat > services.txt
   ```

How it works...

OpenSSL is a tool used for encrypting and decrypting messages, files, and directories. In the preceding example, we used the -base64 scheme. The $-d$ option is used for decryption.

To encrypt a file, we used the $-in$ option, followed by the file that we want to encrypt, and the $-out$ option instructed OpenSSL to store the file. It then stores the encrypted file by the specified name.

7
Writing Bash to Win and Profit

In this chapter, we will introduce the following topics:

- Creating a lame utility HTTP server
- Parsing RSS feeds and output HTML
- Scraping the web and collecting files
- Making a simple IRC chat bot logger
- Blocking IP addresses from failed SSH attempts
- Playing and managing audio from Bash
- Creating a simple NAT and DMZ firewall
- Parsing a GitHub project and generate a report
- Creating a poor man's incremental remote backup
- Using Bash scripts to monitor udev input
- Using Bash to monitor battery life and optimize it
- Using chroot and Restricted Bash shells to secure scripts

Introduction

This chapter will help you learn how to use commands and scripts for many tasks. You will get an idea about writing Bash scripts for monitoring certain tasks. You will learn about hosting files, parsing RSS feeds, and outputing HTML. You will also learn to copy contents from a website, make a simple IRC chat bot logger, block IP addresses, play and manage audio from command line, create a simple NAT firewall with DMZ using iptables, parse GitHub projects, create backups using rsync, monitor device events, the system's battery life and power events, and use chroot for security.

Creating a lame utility HTTP server

In this recipe, we will discuss the cURL tool in Linux. The cURL tool is used for transferring the data from or to a server. It supports many protocols, and `http` is one of them. cURL is used to transfer the data from URL. It has so many tricks to offer, such as http post, ftp post, user authentication, proxy support, file transfer, SSL connections, cookies, and similar.

Getting ready

Besides having a Terminal open, you need to ensure that you have `curl` installed on your system.

How to do it...

We will learn about HTTP GET and POST methods using `curl` in Linux. Now, we will see examples of GET and POST:

1. GET: The HTTP GET method is used to request a data from a specified resource. The command is the example of HTTP GET and is accepting JSON formatted data:

   ```
   $ curl -H "Content-Type:application/json" -H
   "Accept:application/json" -X GET http://host/resource/name
   ```

   Another example of HTTP GET, which is accepting XML formatted data is as follows:

   ```
   $ curl -H "Content-Type:application/xml" -H
   "Accept:application/xml" -X GET http://host/resource/name
   ```

2. POST: The HTTP POST method is used to send the data to server. It is used to create as well as update a resource.

   A simple POST example is as shown:

   ```
   $ curl --data "name1=value1&name2=value2" http://host/resource/name
   ```

   Run the following `curl` command to upload a file:

   ```
   $ curl -T "{File,names,separated,by,comma}"
   http://host/resource/name
   ```

How it works...

Now we will learn about the options used in the curl command:

1. First, we learned about the GET method in the curl command. We accepted two types of data: JSON and XML. We used the -X option and specified the request. -H specifies the header.

2. Second, we learned about the POST method in the curl command. The --data flag is used for the POST request. In the simple example, we are just posting the simple data and in the next, we are uploading files using the -T option.

Parsing RSS feeds and output HTML

In this recipe, we will use the curl and xml2 tools of Linux to parse the RSS feed.

Getting ready

- You need to ensure that you have curl installed on your system
- You need to ensure that you have xml2 installed on your system

How to do it...

We will provide a URL in curl, and using the xml2 tool, we will parse the RSS feed. Run the following command in your Terminal:

```
$ curl -sL https://imdb.com | xml2 | head
```

How it works...

We used xml2 and curl Linux tools to parse the XML RSS feed; xml2 converts XML document into text. In the output, each line is a key that is an XML path, and its value is separated by =.

Scraping the web and collecting files

In this recipe, we will learn how to collect data by web scraping. We will write a script for that.

Getting ready

Besides having a Terminal open, you need to have basic knowledge of the `grep` and `wget` commands.

How to do it...

Now, we will write a script to scrape the contents from `imdb.com`. We will use the `grep` and `wget` commands in the script to get the contents. Create a `scrap_contents.sh` script and write the following code in it:

```
$ mkdir -p data
$ cd data
$ wget -q -r -l5 -x 5  https://imdb.com
$ cd ..
$ grep -r -Po -h '(?<=href=")[^"]*' data/ > links.csv
$ grep "^http" links.csv > links_filtered.csv
$ sort -u links_filtered.csv > links_final.csv
$ rm -rf data links.csv links_filtered.csv
```

How it works...

In the preceding script, we have written code to get contents from a website. The **wget** utility is used for retrieving files from the web using the `http`, `https`, and `ftp` protocols. In this example, we are getting data from `imdb.com` and therefore we specified the website name in `wget`. `grep` is a command-line utility used for searching data that will match a regular expression. Here, we are searching for the specific links, and those links will be saved in `link_final.csv` after the web scraping.

Making a simple IRC chat bot logger

In this recipe, we will make a simple bot logger. This script will log a few channels as well as handle the pings.

Getting ready

Besides having a Terminal open, you need to have basic knowledge of IRC.

How to do it...

Now, we will write a script for an IRC logging bot. Create the `logging_bot.sh` script and write the following code in it:

```
#!/bin/bash
nick="blb$$"
channel=testchannel
server=irc.freenode.net
config=/tmp/irclog
[ -n "$1" ] && channel=$1
[ -n "$2" ] && server=$2
config="${config}_${channel}"
echo "NICK $nick" > $config
echo "USER $nick +i * :$0" >> $config
echo "JOIN #$channel" >> $config
trap "rm -f $config;exit 0" INT TERM EXIT
tail -f $config | nc $server 6667 | while read MESSAGE
do
    case "$MESSAGE" in
        PING*) echo "PONG${MESSAGE#PING}" >> $config;;
*QUIT*) ;;
        *PART*) ;;
        *JOIN*) ;;
        *NICK*) ;;
        *PRIVMSG*) echo "${MESSAGE}" | sed -nr
"s/^:([^!]+).*PRIVMSG[^:]+:(.*)/[$(date '+%R')] \1> \2/p";;
        *) echo "${MESSAGE}";;
    esac
done
```

How it works...

In this script, we handled the pings; also, we are logging some channels.

Blocking IP addresses from failed SSH attempts

In this recipe, we will learn about finding the failed SSH attempts and blocking those IP addresses. To find failed attempts, we will use `grep` as well as `cat` commands. The login attempts to the SSH Server are tracked and recorded into the `rsyslog` daemon.

Getting ready

Besides having a Terminal open, we need to remember a few concepts:

- Basic knowledge of the `grep` and `cat` commands
- Ensure that `grep` is installed

How to do it...

We will find the failed SSH login attempts using the `grep` and `cat` commands. First, be a root user. Type the `sudo su` command. Next, run the following command to fetch the failed attempts using the `grep` command:

```
# grep "Failed password" /var/log/auth.log
```

You can do this using the `cat` command also. Run the following command:

```
# cat /var/log/auth.log | grep "Failed password"
```

You can block the particular IP address that has failed SSH login attempt using tcp-wrapper. Navigate to the `/etc` directory. Look for the `hosts.deny` file, add the following line in the file, and save the file:

```
sshd: 192.168.0.1/255.255.255.0
```

How it works...

In this, we used the `cat` and `grep` commands. The most common use of the `cat` command is to display the contents of a file, and `grep` is a Linux utility used for searching a file for a particular pattern; then, it will display the lines that will have the particular pattern.

In the previous examples, we were searching for a failed login attempt. We are matching such key words using the `grep` command and then we are displaying it using the `cat` command.

To block an IP address, we just added a single line into the `hosts.deny` file, which will block that particular IP address.

Playing and managing audio from Bash

In this recipe, we will learn about how we can play the music from the command-line interface using a command-line player named **SoX**. SoX supports most of the audio formats, such as mp3, wav, mpg, and more.

Getting ready

Besides having a Terminal open, we need to remember a few concepts:

- Ensure that you have SoX installed on your system
- Ensure that you have sox libsox-fmt-all installed

How to do it...

1. We will run the audio from the command line. For that, we will use SoX command-line player. After successful installation of `sox` and `libsox-fmt-all`, navigate to the directory where you have your audio files and run the following command to play all the `.mp3` files:

   ```
   $ play *mp3
   ```

2. To play a specific song, run the following command:

   ```
   $ play file_name.mp3
   ```

How it works...

SoX is used for reading and writing audio files. The `libsox` library is the heart of the SoX tool. The `play` command is used to play the audio files. To play all mp3 files, we used `*mp3`. To play a specific file, just write filename with the extension after the `play` command.

Creating a simple NAT and DMZ firewall

In this recipe, we will create a simple NAT firewall with DMZ using iptables.

Getting ready

Besides having a Terminal open, you need to ensure that `iptables` is installed in your machine.

How to do it...

We will write a script to set up a DMZ using `iptables`. Create a `dmz_iptables.sh` script and write the following code in it:

```
# set the default policy to DROP
iptables -P INPUT DROP
iptables -P OUTPUT DROP
iptables -P FORWARD DROP
# to configure the system as a router, enable ip forwarding by
sysctl -w net.ipv4.ip_forward=1
# allow traffic from internal (eth0) to DMZ (eth2)
iptables -t filter -A FORWARD -i eth0 -o eth2 -m state --state
NEW,ESTABLISHED,RELATED -j ACCEPT
iptables -t filter -A FORWARD -i eth2 -o eth0 -m state --state
ESTABLISHED,RELATED -j ACCEPT
# allow traffic from internet (ens33) to DMZ (eth2)
iptables -t filter -A FORWARD -i ens33 -o eth2 -m state --state
NEW,ESTABLISHED,RELATED -j ACCEPT
iptables -t filter -A FORWARD -i eth2 -o ens33 -m state --state
ESTABLISHED,RELATED -j ACCEPT
#redirect incoming web requests at ens33 (200.0.0.1) of FIREWALL to web
server at 192.168.20.2
iptables -t nat -A PREROUTING -p tcp -i ens33 -d 200.0.0.1 --dport 80 -j
DNAT --to-dest 192.168.20.2
```

```
iptables -t nat -A PREROUTING -p tcp -i ens33 -d 200.0.0.1 --dport 443 -j
DNAT --to-dest 192.168.20.2
#redirect incoming mail (SMTP) requests at ens33 (200.0.0.1) of FIREWALL to
Mail server at 192.168.20.3
iptables -t nat -A PREROUTING -p tcp -i ens33 -d 200.0.0.1 --dport 25 -j
DNAT --to-dest 192.168.20.3
#redirect incoming DNS requests at ens33 (200.0.0.1) of FIREWALL to DNS
server at 192.168.20.4
iptables -t nat -A PREROUTING -p udp -i ens33 -d 200.0.0.1 --dport 53 -j
DNAT --to-dest 192.168.20.4
iptables -t nat -A PREROUTING -p tcp -i ens33 -d 200.0.0.1 --dport 53 -j
DNAT --to-dest 192.168.20.4
```

How it works...

In the preceding code, we have used `iptables` to set up a DMZ. In this script, we are allowing the internal traffic from the internet to the DMZ.

Parsing a GitHub project and generate a report

In this recipe, we will parse a GitHub project using the git command.

Getting ready

Besides having a Terminal open, you need to ensure that you have `git` installed in your system.

How to do it...

We will use the git tool for parsing the project. Run this command to parse a project:

```
$ git https://github.com/torvalds/linux.git
```

How it works...

The tool git is used for handling the large projects. This command is used for cloning the git repository from the server.

Creating a poor man's incremental remote backup

In this recipe, we will learn about creating backups and incremental backups. We will write a script to get incremental backups.

Getting ready

Besides having a Terminal open, we need to remember a few concepts:

- Basic knowledge of the `tar`, `gunzip`, and `gzip` commands.
- Ensure that you have the necessary directories present in your system.

How to do it...

1. First, select a directory whose backup you want to take. We will use the `tar` command. Let's assume that you want to take backup of your `/work` directory:

   ```
   $ tar cvfz work.tar.gz /work
   ```

2. Now, we will write a script to take an incremental backup. Create a `incr_backup.sh` script and write the following code in it:

   ```
   #!/bin/bash
   gunzip /work/tar.gz
   tar uvf /work.tar /work/
   gzip /work.tar
   ```

How it works...

Now, we will learn about the options used in the preceding command as well as the script:

1. In the command, the options we have used are these:
    1. c: This option will create an archive
    2. v: This option is for verbose mode. We can see what files we are archiving.
    3. f: This option will take you back to the file.
    4. z: This option is used to compress it with gzip.
2. In this script, the options we have used are as listed:
    1. u: This option is used for updating the archive.
    2. v: For verbose.
    3. f: This option is to take back to a file.

Using Bash scripts to monitor udev input

In this recipe, we will learn about the **evtest** Linux tool. This tool is used to monitor the input device events.

Getting ready

Besides having a Terminal open, you need to ensure that evtest is installed in your system.

How to do it...

evtest is a command-line tool. It will display the information on the input device. It will display all the events supported by the device. Then, it will monitor the device. We just need to run the evtest command with super user privilege. Run the command as follows:

```
$ sudo evtest /dev/input/event3
```

How it works...

The `evtest` command will produce output as follows:

```
Input driver version is 1.0.1
Input device ID: bus 0x11 vendor 0x2 product 0x13 version 0x6
Input device name: "VirtualPS/2 VMware VMMouse"
Supported events:
  Event type 0 (EV_SYN)
  Event type 1 (EV_KEY)
    Event code 272 (BTN_LEFT)
    Event code 273 (BTN_RIGHT)
  Event type 2 (EV_REL)
    Event code 0 (REL_X)
    Event code 1 (REL_Y)
    Event code 8 (REL_WHEEL)
Properties:
  Property type 0 (INPUT_PROP_POINTER)
Testing ... (interrupt to exit)
```

The output shows the information presented by the kernel.

Using Bash to monitor battery life and optimize it

In this recipe, we will learn about the TLP Linux tool. **TLP** is a command-line tool; it is used for power management and will optimize the battery life.

Getting ready

Besides having a Terminal open, you need to ensure that you have TLP installed on your system.

How to do it...

TLP's configuration file is in the `/etc/default/` directory and the filename is `tlp`. After installation, it starts as a service automatically. We can check whether it's running under system by running the `systemctl` command, as follows:

```
$ sudo systemctl status tlp
```

Run the following command to get the operation mode:

```
$ sudo tlp start
```

To get the system information as well as TLP status, run the following command:

```
$ sudo tlp-stat -s
```

To view TLP configuration, run this command:

```
$ sudo tlp-stat -c
```

To get all the power configurations, run the given command:

```
$ sudo tlp-stat
```

To get the battery information, use this command:

```
$ sudo tlp-stat -b
```

To get the fan speed and temperature of the system, run the next command:

```
$ sudo tlp-stat -t
```

To get the processor data, run the following command:

```
$ sudo tlp-stat -p
```

How it works...

TLP is a command-line tool that comes with automated background tasks. TLP helps in optimizing the battery life in laptops powered by Linux.

We get information about the battery life, processor data, temperature, and fan speed by running `sudo tlp-stat` with various options. `tlp-stat` shows the power management setting. The options we used with `tlp-stat` are as follows:

- `-b`: Battery
- `-t`: Temperature
- `-p`: Processor data
- `-c`: Configuration
- `-s`: System information

Using chroot and restricted Bash shells to secure scripts

In this recipe, we will learn about chroot and restricted bash(rbash). The `chroot` command is used to change the root directory. Using rbash, we can restrict some features of the bash shell for some security purposes.

Getting ready

Besides having a Terminal open, you need to ensure that `rbash` is installed in the system.

How to do it...

1. Now, we will look at the command to start `rbash`. Run the following command:

```
$ bash -r
or
$ rbash
```

2. Now we will test some restrictions. First, we will try to change the directory. Run the following command:

```
$ cd work/
```

Next, we will try to write some contents to the file. Run the given command to write some contents into the file:

```
ls > log.txt
```

How it works...

After using `rbash`, access to the system will be limited. In the preceding examples, we started the restricted shell by typing `bash -r` or `rbash`.

Next, we tried to change the directory, but we got the `rbash: cd: restricted` message, so we cannot change the directory in `rbash`. Also, we cannot write contents into the file.

Advanced Scripting Techniques

8

In this chapter, we will introduce the following recipes:

- Calculating and reducing the runtime of a script
- Writing one-line conditional statements and loops
- Avoiding command not found warnings/errors and improving portability
- Creating a config file and using it in tandem with your scripts
- Improving your shell – GCC and command line colors
- Adding aliases, and altering user paths/variables
- Echoing output to raw terminal devices
- Creating simple frontend GUIs for Bash scripts
- Compiling and installing your own Bash Shell
- Recording terminal sessions for automation
- Writing high-quality scripts by example

Introduction

This chapter will help the readers to learn about advanced scripting techniques as well as how to customize their shell. Users will learn to calculate as well as reduce the runtime of the script. It will be easy for users to write one-line loops and conditional statements. Users will learn to write scripts to avoid warnings and errors. They will learn how to create a config file and use it. Users will learn to improve the shell, adding aliases, altering path variables, and echoing output to terminal devices. Users will also learn about recording terminal sessions and writing scripts.

Calculating and reducing the runtime of a script

In this recipe, we are going to learn how to calculate and reduce the script's runtime. A simple `time` command will help in calculating the execution time.

Getting ready

Besides having a terminal open, make sure you have the necessary scripts present in your system.

How to do it...

Now, we will write a simple script that contains a few commands, and then, using the `time` command, we will get the runtime of that script. Create a script `cal_runtime.sh` and write the following code in it.

```
clear
ls -l
date
sudo apt install python3
```

How it works...

Now, we have written a script `cal_runtime.sh` and four commands in that script: `clear`, `ls`, `date`, and a `python3` installation command. Run your script as follows:

```
$ time bash cal_runtime.sh
```

After the execution, you will get the runtime of the script at the bottom of your output.

Writing one-line conditional statements and loops

In this recipe, we are going to write scripts that will contain one-line conditional statements as well as looping statements.

Getting ready

You need to have basic knowledge of conditional and looping statements.

How to do it...

Now we will write a script for a one-line conditional statement. In this script, we will write a simple `if` condition. Create a script named `if_oneline.sh` and write the following code in it:

```
a=100
if [ $a -eq 100 ]; then echo "a is equal to $a"; fi
```

Next, we will write a script for a one-line `loop` statement. In it, we are going to write a command that will execute 10 times. Create a script `for_online.sh`, and write this code in it.

```
for i in {1..10}; do echo "Hello World"; done
```

Now, we will write a script for a one-line `while` statement. This will be an infinite loop. Create a script named `while_oneline.sh` and write the following code in it:

```
x=10
while [ $x -eq 10 ]; do echo $x; sleep 2; done
```

How it works...

In this recipe, we wrote three scripts for a one-line if statement, for loop, and while loop. In the if example, the condition will be checked and then the output will be displayed on the screen.

In the `for` loop example, the `echo` command will be executed 10 times and Hello world will be displayed 10 times on the screen. In the while example, it will be an infinite loop. We have given a sleep of 2 seconds so that the output, 10, will be executed infinitely every 2 seconds.

Avoiding command not found warnings/errors and improving portability

In this recipe, we are going to learn how to avoid warnings and errors in a shell script. For that, we are going to use the concept of redirection.

Getting ready

Besides having a terminal open, you need to have basic knowledge of the redirection technique.

How to do it...

Sometimes, while debugging your shell scripts, you may not want to view the errors or warning messages as well as your standard output. So for that, we are going to use the redirection technique. Now, we will write `lynda` as a command in our terminal. Run the command as follows.

```
$ lynda
```

```
student@ubuntu:~/Desktop$ lynda
lynda: command not found
student@ubuntu:~/Desktop$
```

You will get the `command not found` error. We can avoid this error by running the following command.

```
$ lynda 2> log.txt
```

We will write a script with a wrong syntax for declaring the variable. And we will redirect that error message to `log.txt`. Create a script `avoid_error.sh`, and write following content in it.

```
echo "Hello World"
a = 100
b=20
c=$((a+b))
echo $a
```

In the second line, `a = 100`, we will get an error.

How it works...

Whatever error message you get after pressing *Enter*, that error will get stored in log.txt. Now view the contents of log.txt as follows:

```
$ cat log.txt
```

```
student@ubuntu:~/Desktop$ lynda 2> log.txt
student@ubuntu:~/Desktop$ cat log.txt
lynda: command not found
student@ubuntu:~/Desktop$
```

So, in this way, you can avoid warnings as well as errors. Now, run the script as:

```
$ bash avoid_error.sh 2> log.txt
```

The error message will get stored in log.txt. You can view it by running the cat log.txt command.

Creating a config file and using it in tandem with your scripts

In this recipe, we are going to create a config file and use it in our shell script.

Getting ready

Besides having a terminal open, you need basic knowledge of creating scripts and config files.

How to do it...

Now, we are going to create a script and config file. The extension of the configuration file is .conf. Create a script called sample_script.sh and write this code in it:

```
#!/bin/bash
typeset -A config
config=(
    [username]="student"
    [password]=""
```

```
        [hostname]="ubuntu"
)
while read line
do
    if echo $line | grep -F = &>/dev/null
    then
        varname=$(echo "$line" | cut -d '=' -f 1)
        config[$varname]=$(echo "$line" | cut -d '=' -f 2-)
    fi
done < sampleconfig.conf
echo ${config[username]}
echo ${config[password]}
echo ${config[hostname]}
echo ${config[PROMPT_COMMAND]}
```

We will now create a configuration file. Create a file called `sampleconfig.conf` and write the following code in it:

```
password=training
echo rm -rf /
PROMPT_COMMAND='ls -l'
hostname=ubuntu; echo rm -rf /
```

How it works...

After running the script username, password, and hostname, it will display the command we mentioned in `PROMPT_COMMAND`.

Improving your shell – GCC and command line colors

In this recipe, we are going learn how a user can improve the shell. We will do this using the PS1 bash environment variable.

Getting ready

Besides a terminal, you need basic knowledge of PS1.

How to do it...

The terminal appearance is taken by the `PS1` shell variable. The content allowed in `PS1` will contain backslash-escape special characters.

First, we will see what PS1's current contents in the system. For that, run the following command:

```
$ echo $PS1
```

```
student@ubuntu:~$ echo $PS1
\[\e]0;\u@\h: \w\a\]${debian_chroot:+($debian_chroot)}\[\033[01;32m\]\u@\h\[\033
[00m\]:\[\033[01;34m\]\w\[\033[00m\]\$
student@ubuntu:~$
```

Here are the backslash-escape special characters:

- `\u`: Current username
- `\h`: Hostname
- `\W`: Current working directory
- `\$`: Will display # if the user is root; otherwise it will display $ only
- `\@`: Current time in 12-hour AM/PM format

Now, we will modify our Bash. Run the following command:

```
$ PS1="[\\u@\\h \\W \\@]\\$"
```

```
[student@ubuntu Desktop 03:56 PM]$
[student@ubuntu Desktop 03:56 PM]$PS1="[\\u@\\h \\W \\@]\\$"
[student@ubuntu Desktop 03:56 PM]$
```

Now, we will write a command to change the colors.

To make the text color blue, run the following command:

```
$ PS1="[\\u@\\h \\W \\@]\\$\\e[0;34m"
```

```
[student@ubuntu Desktop 03:56 PM]$PS1="[\\u@\\h \\W \\@]\\$\\e[0;34m"
[student@ubuntu Desktop 03:59 PM]$
[student@ubuntu Desktop 03:59 PM]$echo "Hello World"
Hello World
[student@ubuntu Desktop 03:59 PM]$
```

Now we, will see the `tput` command. Run the following commands:

```
$ PS1="\[$(tput setaf 3)\]\u@\h:\w $ \[$(tput sgr0)\]"
```

```
student@ubuntu:~ $ PS1="\[$(tput setaf 3)\]\u@\h:\w $ \[$(tput sgr0)\]"
student@ubuntu:~ $
student@ubuntu:~ $
```

```
$ PS1="\[$(tput setaf 6)\]\u@\h:\w $ \[$(tput sgr0)\]"
```

```
student@ubuntu:~ $ PS1="\[$(tput setaf 6)\]\u@\h:\w $ \[$(tput sgr0)\]"
student@ubuntu:~ $
student@ubuntu:~ $ _
```

How it works...

We used the `PS1` shell variable to improve our shell. We add colors in the `PS1` variable and the colors were changed. We used the `tput` command too. This command is also used to modify the settings. `setaf` sets the foreground color, and `setab` sets the background color. The color codes for the `tput` command are as follows:

Code	Color
0	Black
1	Red
2	Green
3	Yellow
4	Blue
5	Magenta
6	Cyan
7	White

Adding aliases, and altering user paths/variables

In this recipe, we are going to create an alias of a command and alter the user path variable. We are going to learn about the `alias` command. Using `alias` command, we are going to create aliases for other commands.

Getting ready

Besides having a terminal open, we need the basic knowledge of the alias command.

How to do it...

1. We will create a alias for the `pwd` command. Run this command:

```
$ alias p=pwd
```

2. Now, we will create an alias for the `ls` command. Run the following command:

```
$ alias l="ls -l"
```

How it works...

The `alias` command is used to create a shortcut for commonly used commands.

1. We have created an alias p for command `pwd`. So, we just run the p command to get the present working directory.
2. We have created an alias l for command `ls`. So, we just run the l command to get the list.

Echoing output to raw terminal devices

In this recipe, we are going to learn how we can echo the output from one terminal to another. To achieve this, we are going to use `tty`.

Getting ready

Besides having a terminal open, you need basic knowledge of `tty`.

How to do it...

tty means **teletype.** `tty` displays terminal-related information. Everything in Linux is a file. So, `tty` prints the filename of the terminal that is connected to standard input.

Now, open a terminal and run tty:

```
$ tty
```

After running this command, the current `tty` session will be displayed.

Open another terminal B and do the same; you will get that terminal's tty session.

Now I have two tty sessions as:

- Terminal A = `/dev/pts/4`
- Terminal B = `/dev/pts/7`

In Terminal A, run the following command:

```
$ echo "Hello World" > /dev/pts/7
```

Now check Terminal B; `Hello world` will be displayed on the terminal. Again, run the following command to send another string to terminal B.

```
$ echo "Hello This is John" > /dev/pts/7
```

How it works...

The following will be the output on terminal B.

```
Hello World
Hello This is John
```

Creating simple frontend GUIs for Bash scripts

In this recipe, we are going to create a simple GUI. We are going to use the zenity tool to do so.

Getting ready

Besides having a terminal open, make sure you have zenity installed in your system.

How to do it...

Zenity is used to add a graphical interface to shell scripts using a single command. Zenity comes by default with Ubuntu. If not, then install it as follows:

```
$ sudo apt install zenity
```

First, we will catch a yes/no response in our shell script and then perform different commands based on the button. Run the following command to get the yes/no response.

```
$ zenity --question --title="Query" --text="Would you like to run the
script?"
```

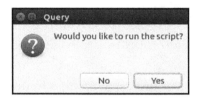

Run the following command to get the error message box:

```
$ zenity --error --title="An Error Occurred" --text="A problem occurred
while running the shell script."
```

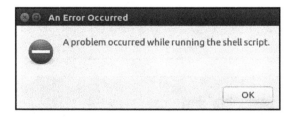

Run the following command to get the text entry:

```
$ zenity --entry --title="Favorite Website" --text="What is your favorite website?"
```

Now we will create a script where the user has to enter a time and till that time the user has to wait. When the wait is over, the user will get a message. Create a script, user_wait.sh, and write the following content in it.

```
#!/bin/bash
time=$(zenity --entry --title="Timer" --text="Enter a duration for the timer.\n\n Use 10s for 10 seconds, 20m for 20 minutes, or 3h for 3 hours.")
sleep $time
zenity --info --title="Timer Complete" --text="The timer is over.\n\n It has been $time."
```

Use 10s for 10 seconds, 20m for 20 minutes, or 3h for 3 hours as shown in the following screenshots:

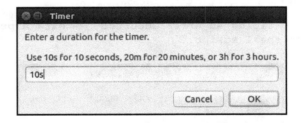

The timer is over:

How it works...

Zenity is an open source application that displays dialog boxes using shell scripts as well as the command line. Using zenity communication between the user and shell will be easy:

- --question: Displays question dialog box
- --error: Displays error dialog box
- --entry: Displays text entry dialog box
- --info: Displays info dialog box

In the script user_wait.sh, we are creating a Timer using a text entry dialogbox and info dialogbox. We have created a variable named time. We are asking the user to enter a duration of time and that value will be stored in the time variable. Then we are providing that variable to sleep. Therefore, until that time, the user has to wait. After the time completes, the user will get the information dialogbox as the time is over.

Compiling and installing your own Bash shell

In this recipe, we are going to learn about compile and install the Bash shell. We are going to use SHC, which is shell script compiler.

Getting ready

Besides having a terminal open, make sure you have SHC installed in your system.

How to do it...

Now we will write a simple shell script that will print "Hello World". Using SHC, the Shell script will be converted into binaries directly. Create a script hello.sh, and write the following content in it.

```
#!/bin/bash
echo "Hello World"
a=10
b=20
c=$((a+b))
echo $c
```

Now, to log all commands, run the logger command as follows:

```
$ logger -f hello.sh
```

How it works...

After executing the script, two extra files will be created. The files are:

- hello.sh.x: This file is the stripped binary encrypted shell script in binary format
- hello.sh.x.c: This file is the C source code of hello.sh

Now, execute the encrypted shell script as follows:

```
$ ./hello.sh.x
```

The logger command will make an entry about your file in the syslog file, which is present in the /var/log directory of your system. You can check out that file. Navigate to /var/log directory and run nano syslog; you will find the entry in it.

Recording terminal sessions for automation

In this recipe, we are going to learn how to record terminal sessions. We are going to use the **ttyrec** tool to do this.

Getting ready

Besides having a Terminal open, make sure ttyrec is installed in your system.

How to do it...

To record terminal data, we use the ttyrec tool. You can also play the recorded data. Now, to record the terminal session, enter the `ttyrec` command in the terminal. You can end the recording by typing `exit`. Run the following command to record the terminal session:

```
$ ttyrec
```

How it works...

When you run the `ttyrec` command, the terminal record session will be started. The recording will go on until you type exit. As soon as you type `exit`, the recording will be stopped and a file will be created in your current working directory. The filename will be `ttyrecord`. You can play this file by running the `ttyplay` command. Run the `ttyrecord` file as follows:

```
$ ttyplay ttyrecord
```

Writing high-quality scripts by example

In this recipe, we are going to see functions in shell scripts. We will see how our program testing is done, sequentially on the various parts, using functions. Functions help improve the readability of a program.

Getting ready

Besides having a terminal open, you need to have a basic knowledge of functions.

How to do it...

We are going to write a simple function in our shell script to return the current date and time. Create a script `function_example.sh`, and write this code in it:

```
#!/bin/bash
print_date()
{
echo "Today is `date`"
return
}
print_date
```

Now we will create another script containing two functions with the same name. Create a script `function2.sh`, and write the following content in it.

```
#!/bin/bash
display ( ) {
echo 'First Block'
echo 'Number 1'
}
display ( ) {
echo 'Second Block'
echo 'Number 2'
}
display
exit 0
```

How it works...

In the first script, we created a function named `print_date()` and we just printed a date using a function.

In the second script, we wrote two functions with the same name. However, after execution, the last value was printed on the screen. So in this case, **Second block Number 2** will be printed on the screen.

Other Books You May Enjoy

If you enjoyed this book, you may be interested in these other books by Packt:

Mastering Bash
Giorgio Zarrelli

ISBN: 978-1-78439-687-9

- Understand Bash right from the basics and progress to an advanced level
- Customize your environment and automate system routine tasks
- Write structured scripts and create a command-line interface for your scripts
- Understand arrays, menus, and functions
- Securely execute remote commands using ssh
- Write Nagios plugins to automate your infrastructure checks
- Interact with web services, and a Slack notification script
- Find out how to execute subshells and take advantage of parallelism
- Explore inter-process communication and write your own daemon

Mastering Linux Shell Scripting - Second Edition
Mokhtar Ebrahim, Andrew Mallett

ISBN: 978-1-78899-055-4

- Make, execute, and debug your first Bash script
- Create interactive scripts that prompt for user input
- Foster menu structures for operators with little command-line experience
- Develop scripts that dynamically edit web configuration files to produce a new virtual host
- Write scripts that use AWK to search and reports on log files
- Draft effective scripts using functions as building blocks, reducing maintenance and build time
- Make informed choices by comparing different script languages such as Python with Bash

Leave a review - let other readers know what you think

Please share your thoughts on this book with others by leaving a review on the site that you bought it from. If you purchased the book from Amazon, please leave us an honest review on this book's Amazon page. This is vital so that other potential readers can see and use your unbiased opinion to make purchasing decisions, we can understand what our customers think about our products, and our authors can see your feedback on the title that they have worked with Packt to create. It will only take a few minutes of your time, but is valuable to other potential customers, our authors, and Packt. Thank you!

Index

A

alarm
  generating 194, 195
alias command 230, 231
aliases
  adding 230
apt command 197
arrays 69
artefact 81
artifact 81
ASCII 43
audio
  managing 215, 216
  playing 215, 216
AWK
  used, for replacing substrings 71, 75

B

Bash script
  creating, with Vim 11, 12, 13
  simple frontend GUIs, creating for 233, 234
  used, for monitoring udev input 219, 220
Bash shell
  compiling 235, 236
  installing 235, 236
Bash
  about 41
  battery life, monitoring 220
  fundamentals 8, 9, 11
  strings, managing 61
basic loops
  about 24
  do while loop 25
  for loop 24
basic network connectivity
  configuring 177, 178

battery life
  monitoring, Bash used 220
binary numbers
  evaluating 20
binary
  about 76
  dependencies, finding 205, 206
bzip2 182

C

calculations
  in scripts 55, 56, 57, 60
case statement
  about 23
  creating 23
cat command 214
chroot
  used, for securing scripts 222
CLI
  graphics, creating on 197, 198
  presentations, creating on 197, 198
  web, browsing from 202, 203
Comma Separated Values (CSV) 96
command line colors 229
command not found warnings/errors
  avoiding 226, 227
commands
  about 38
  invoking, on permission requirement 142, 143,
    144, 145, 146
  linking 32
conditional logic
  file attributes, using with 90, 92, 93, 94, 96
  using 19
config file
  creating 227, 228
  using, in shell script 227, 228

configuration
   adding, to /etc/logrotate.d/ 183
connectivity diagnostics 176, 177
Cron Jobs
   configuring 190
   creating 190
crontab command 191
curl command 211

D

data
   formatting, echo used 76
   formatting, printf used 76
datasets
   generating 131, 132, 134
date command 206
dd command
   using 196
delimited data
   reading 96, 97, 98, 99
delimiters 96
dialog command 197
diff
   creating, of two files 111, 112, 113, 114, 115
directories
   monitoring 179
dmidecode tool 172
DMZ firewall
   creating 216, 217
do while loop 25
duplicate directories
   deleting 124, 125
   finding 122
duplicate files
   deleting 124
   finding 122, 123
duplicates
   reducing, based on file contents 87, 88, 90

E

echo
   data, formatting 76
   output, formatting 76
elif statement 19
ELinks 202

else statement 19
encoding scheme 43
escape character 18
evtest tool 219
extension
   files, searching by 106, 108, 109, 110
external functions
   using 28

F

failed SSH attempts
   IP addresses, blocking from 214, 215
file attributes
   using, with conditional logic 90, 92, 93, 94, 96
file descriptor
   reference 34
file integrity
   checking for 199
file-in-file-out program
   creating 162, 163, 164
files
   archiving 179, 180, 181
   basic searching 43, 44, 45
   collecting 212
   compressing 179, 180, 181
   decrypting, from script 207
   encrypting, from script 207
   generating, of multiple sizes 131, 132, 134
   joining, at arbitrary positions 126, 127, 129, 130
   monitoring 179
   new configuration directives 184
   retrieving 201, 202
   searching, by name/extension 106, 108, 109, 111
   splitting, at arbitrary positions 126, 127, 128, 129, 130
   viewing, from various angles 102, 103, 104, 106
filesystem directories
   crawling 119, 120, 121
firewall
   Linux IPtables, using for 184, 185, 186
float 14
for loop
   about 24
   functions, using with parameters 27

format 43
functions
  using 25

G

git command 217
GitHub project
  parsing 217, 218
global context 17
globbing 48
graphics
  creating, on CLI 197, 198
grep command 33, 45, 214
groups
  creating 192

H

head command 102
headers
  including 27
here-string 60
hexadecimal 76
hidden variables 17, 18
high-quality scripts
  writing 237, 238
HTTP GET method 210
HTTP POST method 210
hunk 115

I

if statement 19
incremental remote backup
  creating 218, 219
inotify 179
inotifywait command 179
integer 14
integrated development editors (IDEs) 11
internationalization
  script, reading for languages 80, 81, 83, 85, 86
inverted logic 47
IP addresses
  blocking, from failed SSH attempts 214, 215
iptables 184
iwconfig command 32

J

jobs 140

L

lame utility HTTP server
  creating 210, 211
less command 102
library script
  importing 28
  including 28
Linux IPtables
  using, for firewall 184, 185, 186
literal string 14
log files
  managing 183, 184
logrotate command 183
logs
  files, rotating from RAM to storage 182
loops
  until loop 25
  writing 224, 225
Lorem Ipsum 104
ls command 9

M

man command 38
math
  in scripts 55, 56, 57, 60
MD5sum 122
media file
  backing up 196
  erasing 196
more command 102
mount command 201

N

name
  files, searching by 106, 108, 109
named pipes 163
nested conditional statements 22
network file systems
  mounting 201, 202
network information
  gathering 176, 177

network traffic
  capturing, headlessly 203, 204

O

one-line conditional statements
  writing 224, 225
OpenSSL 208
output format
  altering 96, 97, 98, 99
output HTML 211
output
  echoing, to raw terminal devices 231, 232
  retrieving 29

P

parameters
  using 26
passwordless remote access
  SSH keys, creating for 189, 190
patch 112
patching 113, 115
pattern 43
pipes 35, 162
play command 216
portability
  improving 226, 227
presentations
  creating, on CLI 197, 198
printf
  data, formatting 76
  output, formatting 76
processes
  running, in parallel 162, 163, 164, 165
program flags
  passing 36, 37
program input parameters
  obtaining 35
programs
  keeping running, after logoff 139, 140, 141, 142
  lock files, using 156, 157, 158
  temporary files, using 156, 157, 158
pwd command 9

R

raw terminal devices
  output, echoing to 231, 232
readarray command 69
recursive functionality 42
redirection 34
regexes
  reference 54
  using 48, 49, 50, 51, 53, 54
report
  generating 217
reserved words
  about 17
  reference 18
restricted Bash shells
  used, for securing scripts 222
return codes 101 30, 31
return codes
  retrieving 29
root user 8
RSS feeds
  parsing 211

S

scope 13
scp command 202
scripts
  executing, on startup 165, 166, 168, 169
  files, decrypting from 207
  files, encrypting from 207
  keeping running, after logoff 139, 140, 141, 142
  running, indefinitely 136, 137, 138, 139
  runtime, calculating 224
  runtime, reducing 224
  securing, chroot used 222
  securing, restricted Bash shells used 222
Select
  used, for making simple user menu 151, 152, 154
SHA512sum 122
shell script
  about 9
  config file, using in 227, 228
shell

about 8
improving 228, 229, 230
SIGHUP 154
sign 60
signals
  generating 154, 155, 156
  trapping, for cleanup 154, 155, 156
simple frontend GUIs
  creating, for Bash scripts 232, 234
simple IRC chat bot logger
  making 213, 214
simple NAT firewall
  creating 216, 217
source files
  including 27
SoX 215
SQL databases
  accessing, locally 186, 188
  accessing, remotely 186, 188
SSH keys
  creating, for passwordless remote access 189,
    190
statistics
  calculating 87, 88, 89
stream editor (SED)
  about 70
  used, for removing substrings 71, 73
strings
  about 14
  altering 62, 63, 65, 67, 69
  basic searching 43, 44, 45
  deleting 66
  evaluating 21
  searching 67
  sorting 62, 63, 64
  striping 62, 64
substitute user do (Sudo) 142
substrings
  removing, SED used 71, 73
  replacing, AWK used 71, 75
switch statement
  creating 23
symbolic links
  creating 116, 117
  using 117, 118

Syslog entries
  creating 194, 195
system information
  aggregating 172, 174, 175
  gathering 172, 174, 175

T
tail command 32, 102
tampering
  checking for 199
TAR file 182
tcpdump 203
terminal 8
terminal sessions
  recording, for automation 237
time command 224
time
  fetching, from different locations 206, 207
timeout
  leveraging, on wait for command completion
    159, 160, 161
TLP 220, 221
tree
  printing 119, 120, 121
ttyrec tool 237

U
udev input
  monitoring, Bash scripts used 219, 220
until loop 25
user input
  sanitizing 147, 149, 150, 151
user menu
  making, Select used 151, 152, 154
user paths
  altering 230
useradd command 192
users
  creating 191
UTF 43

V
variable assignment 15, 16
variables
  altering 230

creating 13
hidden variables 18
using 13
Vim
  Bash script, creating 11, 12, 13
  reference 13

W

W3M 202
web
  browsing, from CLI 202, 203

scraping 212
wget utility 212
whoami command 9
wildcards
  using 47, 49, 50, 51
wpa_supplicant 177

Z

zenity tool
  about 232
  working 235
zip 182

www.ingramcontent.com/pod-product-compliance
Lightning Source LLC
Chambersburg PA
CBHW080634060326
40690CB00021B/4928

9781788629362